HEART BAGS & HAND SHAKES

The Story of the Cook Collection

Other books by Dorothy Cook Meade –

History of the Agate Post Office (1988)
The Story of Agate Springs Ranch (1990)

Front Cover (left):
Three significant heart bags in the Cook Collection are shown. The center bag belonged to Oglala Sioux Chief Red Cloud. To its right is the bag belonging to Red Cloud's son, Jack Red Cloud; and on the far left is the heart bag which belonged to Red Cloud's father. These bags were used to hold pipe and smoking materials. They were called "heart bags" because, when the pipes were smoked, the Sioux were obligated always to speak "from the heart."
Photo courtesy NEBRASKAland Magazine, Nebraska Game and Parks Commission.

Front Cover (right):
Three of the many pipes from the Cook Collection are illustrated in this photograph. All three have bowls carved from catlinite, or "pipestone," a soft clay-like stone containing iron which gives it a rust color. The pipe bowl on the left is inlaid with polished lead.
Photo courtesy NEBRASKAland Magazine, Nebraska Game and Parks Commission.

Heart Bags & Hand Shakes

THE STORY OF THE COOK COLLECTION

DOROTHY COOK MEADE

NATIONAL WOODLANDS PUBLISHING COMPANY

Lake Ann, Michigan

Photos courtesy of:

    Agate Fossil Beds National Monument, National Park Service, U.S. Department of the Interior

    NEBRASKAland Magazine, Nebraska Game and Parks Commission

Book design by Jim•Dew•Art•Do•Art

HEART BAGS & HAND SHAKES
The Story of the Cook Collection

© 1994 by Dorothy Cook Meade

First Edition: June 1994

Publisher's Cataloging in Publication Data

Meade, Dorothy Cook.
    Heart bags & hand shakes: the story of the Cook Collection/Dorothy Cook Meade
    p. cm.
    Includes bibliographical references.
    Preassigned LCCN: 94-066130
    ISBN 0-9628075-4-0
    1. Indians of North America-Sioux. 2. Indians of North America-Cheyenne.

94 95 96 97 98   10 9 8 7 6 5 4 3 2 1

To all the Indian friends,
Sioux and Cheyenne,
whose generosity made it possible
for James Cook
to form the Cook Collection.

Was-te, was-te, mita cola
(Good, good, my friend)

Among the many Indian friends who visited James Cook at Agate Springs Ranch over the years were these men: Oglala Sioux Chief Red Cloud (lower left), Red Cloud's son, Jack Red Cloud (upper right), Knife Chief (upper left), and Baptiste "Little Bat" Garnier (right front). The latter was half French and half Sioux. On many occasions, they brought gifts for Cook and his family and the gifts became part of the Cook Collection. Photo taken in the mid- to late-1890s.

CONTENTS

Most of the black-and-white photographs displayed in this book are from the Cook family archives and have been supplied by the author or by the National Park Service. Where known, the photographer's name is provided. Thirteen photographs of specific items in the collection have been produced from color prints and slides taken by Bob Grier. These include the following: leggings, page 29; little boy's suit, page 32; all three photos, page 35; two small photos, page 39; all three photos, page 47; all three photos, page 51. Those photographs are also part of the archival files at Agate Fossil Beds National Monument.

The color photographs in the book are from several sources. Reid Miller, former Park Ranger at Agate Fossil Beds National Monument, took the picture of the five small bags and pouches which is shown on page 42. Bob Grier took all of the other photos. Some (Front Cover, pages 21 and 23) previously appeared in the March 1988 issue of *NEBRASKAland* Magazine. The others are part of the permanent catalog files at Agate Fossil Beds National Monument.

*I*n October 1935, I was stationed at Yellowstone National Park as a temporary ranger, filling in for permanent rangers on vacation. One day, I got a telephone call from the Chief Ranger's office, and someone read to me a telegram from Washington, D.C. It told me to report without delay to Scotts Bluff National Monument in western Nebraska as its first full-time, paid "Custodian." Upon arrival there I was impressed by two things: the giant bluff made famous by the diaries of emigrants over the old Oregon-California Trail, and, secondly, the wealth of Oligocene fossils exposed in these bluffs. Soon I learned that my predecessor at Scotts Bluff was Harold Cook, then in residence at a place called Agate Springs Ranch, some fifty miles northward. I soon made a pilgrimage up there to confer with him about Scotts Bluff's history and paleon-

tology. When I arrived at Agate, more wonders were revealed.

Harold Cook was, himself, a paleontologist, and his ranch embraced not only extensive grasslands but also the world famous Agate Fossil Quarries. At the ranch house was Harold's father, James H. Cook, builder of the ranch and himself famous for his frontier exploits, his association with the old Agate ranch, and his fabulous collection of Sioux and Cheyenne Indian artifacts. He regaled me with stories about the annual visits of Chief Red Cloud and his folk to the ranch to honor their old friend and bestow gifts upon him. It seems that he had befriended the famous chief and his followers, and this led to his amazing collection of Indian artifacts – tomahawks, scalping knives, rifles, hide paintings, etc.

Subsequently, a new western trails museum at Scotts Bluff National

Monument opened in 1936 and later was expanded by the Civilian Conservation Corps to include a paleontology wing. It contained specimens collected by CCC boys led by paleontologist Paul McGrew. The display included magnificent specimens from the Agate quarries. When in later years the quarries themselves were dedicated as a National Monument, the Scotts Bluff paleontological exhibits were transferred back to that new area. At the same time, James Cook's Indian collection was stored at Scotts Bluff National Monument pending development of a museum at Agate. With such a museum now a reality, the history-paleontology wheel of Scotts Bluff/Agate Fossil Quarries has come full circle.

While the near half-century I have lived since leaving Scotts Bluff in 1946 has involved me in research, planning, restoration and reconstruction in many other western historical areas – e.g., Fort Laramie and Bent's Old Fort – I will always remember my halcyon days involving the majestic Scotts Bluffs and the old Agate Springs Ranch with its famous quarries and collection of Indian artifacts.

Among other things I remember from those early days is that Harold Cook had four young daughters. One of the two who survive is Dorothy – Mrs. Grayson E. Meade – who has lived at Agate Springs Ranch since 1972. She has written this book to record the personal history that is attached to many of the objects in the Cook Collection. It is history that the Indian friends who gave James Cook the objects asked that he remember and

share with others. This he did during his lifetime. Dorothy Cook Meade writes this account from her own perspective, based on recollections of her early years of living at Agate and of her associations with her grandfather, James Cook. Her intent in writing this book is to continue her grandfather's and her father's dedication to preserving these Indian artifacts as well as honoring those who bestowed them upon the Cook family. I believe readers will gain an appreciation for how special the Cook Collection is, particularly its place in history.

MERRILL J. MATTES
Retired Chief of Historic Preservation
Denver Service Center, National Park Service
U.S. Department of the Interior

ACKNOWLEDGMENTS

As readers will find, this book provides a personal perspective of the Cook Collection of Sioux and Cheyenne Indian artifacts. These recollections date back to my childhood and early youth. My grandfather, James H. Cook, and my parents, Harold and Eleanor Cook, developed in their children an appreciation of the Indian artifacts and the stories that accompanied them. To an unusual degree, the energy, enthusiasm, and patience they showed through the years, while repeatedly telling those stories, made indelible impressions on my mind. Though they are long gone, I am most grateful for the legacy of memories they left me.

The National Park Service provided significant help while I was preparing the manuscript and I am most apprecia-tive. For providing access to documents, tapes, and photographs that would not otherwise have been available to me, I particularly thank Reid Miller, Park Ranger who was stationed at Agate Fossil Beds National Monument, and Mark Hertig, Museum Specialist, also at Agate Fossil Beds.

My sister, Winifred C. McGrew, read and commented helpfully on an early version of the manuscript. I am also grateful to Victoria White, a Cheyenne friend, for her insight. I have been privileged to know three of Chief Red Cloud's great-great granddaughters. They are Sadie Janice, Nancy Horn Cloud, and Zona Fills the Pipe. Without their generous help, I would have had great difficulty identifying many of the Indian visitors to Agate who appear in old photographs.

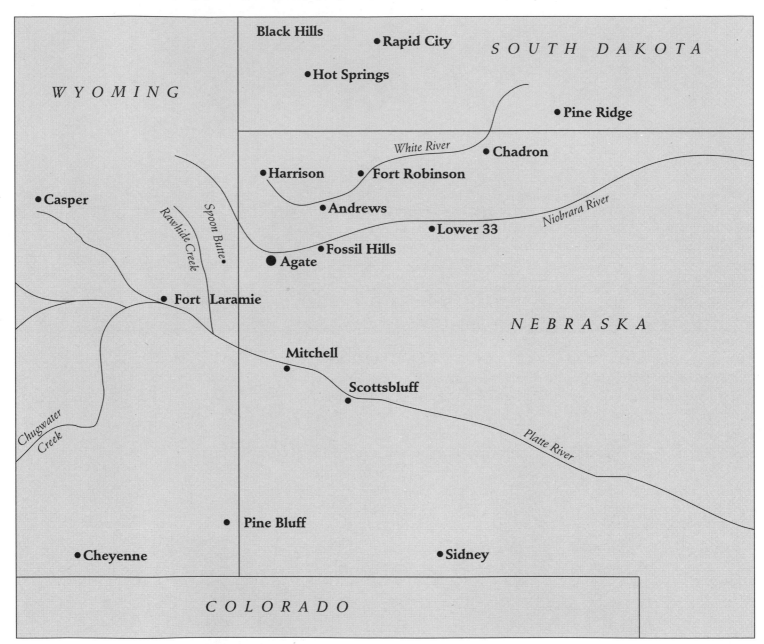

*L*ittle love was lost between white men and Indians anywhere on this continent one hundred years ago, least of all in the West. Throughout the history of white men's intrusion upon Indian lands, warriors had defended their hunting grounds ferociously. They harried wagon trains, disrupted settlements and killed settlers. In retaliating, the Army was often as brutal as the tribes. The memory of the climactic battle of the Little Bighorn, where Custer and his entire command were wiped out, was still painfully recent a century ago. Remembering Custer, few white people believed any friendship possible with Indian leaders. Fewer still were the Indian leaders who cared to seek such friendship.

Yet, against all likelihood, a frontiersman named James Cook became friends with many old-time warriors, leaders of the Sioux and Cheyenne. As we shall see, the bonds they formed were already well established before the Custer battle of 1876. By 1887, Cook had settled on a ranch of his own in northwest Nebraska. At once, he invited his Indian friends to visit him there. They got permission to leave their reservations and came, sometimes in large numbers. The Cooks supplied their guests with beef, garden vegetables, and staples during the visits. Their Indian friends, who, according to their own traditions, never came empty-handed, brought gifts of all sorts. From these, a collection of Indian artifacts gradually grew and today commands unusual interest.

Personal histories rarely remain attached to individual artifacts in a museum. In the Cook Collection, however, many artifacts are linked to historic persons and events. Because of the unusual friendship that existed, the history of each article was recounted to James Cook as it was given to him.

Cook stored the information in his memory and retold it many times.

All this came about after Jim Cook met Baptiste (Little Bat) Garnier at Fort Laramie, Wyoming, in 1875. Garnier, half French and half Sioux, was a scout for the U.S. Army who nevertheless maintained close ties with his Sioux relatives. Jim Cook, then a youth of 18, was a cowboy employed on Ben Slaughter's ranch in south Texas. Cook had completed a drive of longhorn cattle from Texas to Abilene, Kansas, when he decided to visit Fort Laramie. While there he met Garnier and the two struck up a friendship. They were much the same age and both were avid hunters. After camping and hunting together for a time, Little Bat suggested that Cook go with him on a trip to visit the Red Cloud Agency in Nebraska, near the site of present-day Crawford.

There, Little Bat introduced Cook to Red Cloud. He told the Chief that Cook was both a friend and a hunter who was familiar with the country from the Shell River (the North Platte) to the southern ocean. Red Cloud welcomed them and sent out word for some of his greatest sub-chiefs and warriors to come to his lodge. On that occasion, Cook met for the first time many of the old, "wild" Indians who later became his friends and remained so for as long as they lived.

Cook was able that day to give helpful advice on a question that troubled the Indians. The paleontologist O.C. Marsh, of Yale University, was camped nearby and was requesting permission to collect fossils in Sioux territory. Many Indian leaders thought Marsh was actually looking for gold, so they favored refusal of his request. Cook offered to speak with Marsh to learn what he could. Soon Cook was able to assure Red Cloud and the others that Marsh meant only to look for "stone bones" and not for "yellow lead."

As a result, Marsh was given permission to do his collecting. A strong friendship formed between Marsh and the Indians as he found ways to help the chiefs in their problems with government agents. Later, when Red Cloud made a trip to the East, he and Marsh were photographed shaking hands, a pipe of peace between them. James Cook, in turn, came to be known as a man whose word they could trust.

Cook's sympathy for the Indian point of view was striking for his time. He admired the superb skills mastered by Sioux and Cheyenne in their lives on the plains. He saw them as individuals with honorable histories, each of whom had fully earned his title as Chief, Orator, or Medicine Man through his own demonstrated wisdom and courage. Changes then visibly overtaking the West were almost as painful to Cook as they were to the Indians: the pristine land filling with settlers, wildlife vanishing, and tribes confined to reservations. When the Indians asked for his counsel, Cook's advice to them was based on respect and desire for their well-being. His outlook was remarkable at a time when most white people agreed that the only good Indian was a dead Indian.

For the Indians, it was a time of upheaval unlike any they had ever known. The old, wild days were over. The vast herds of bison on which their livelihood was based had vanished. Well-honed skills, essential to a life of hunting and warfare, became useless now that they were confined to reservations and forbidden to hunt. Their young people, overwhelmed by change, neglected former customs. Many of the most able of them were away, enlivening Wild West shows with their presence, traveling widely, and giving the world what inevitably was a distorted view of the old West. All the while, they were growing personally more unsuited to their former lives.

The elders mourned these changes. They feared that all their ways would be forgotten and their most meaningful possessions would be scattered after they were gone. Hoping to avoid this fate, the old chiefs placed their treasures in the hands of their friend, James Cook, to keep in his ranch home at Agate. They said they trusted him to keep the belongings safe and to remember the tales that went with them. In this spirit, Red Cloud brought the worn old pipe bag that was the last thing he had from his father, as well as his own splendid one, and that of his son, Jack. American Horse dictated a will, leaving his quilled shirt to Cook; and Little Chief gave Cook the very gun that his son had been carrying when he was killed during the desperate Cheyenne break-out from Fort Robinson in 1879.

As a friend, Cook had taken pains to learn the Sioux language and attempt to understand their ways, demonstrating a degree of interest they had not encountered elsewhere. Cook, too, had come to dread the thought that the old Indian customs might soon all be forgotten. He felt an urgent need to preserve, somewhere in the world, a clear picture

Agate Springs Ranch about 1898. Corrals, foreground. Ranch house among the trees. Indian encampment at the right.

4

*Red Cloud, Chief of the Oglala Sioux Nation. Official U.S.
Government photograph made in 1875 with a glass plate negative.*

of what their former lives had been.

Beyond the ability of objects in his collection to summon up memories of old friendships, Cook valued them for their historical significance, beauty, and utility. Even the most humble object illuminated for him a way of life, successful for centuries, that was now slipping into the past. Cook felt great obligation to preserve what remained of that life as expressed by its garments, tools, and weapons, and the customs they reflected. He often spoke of his collection as "priceless," and he was not thinking of dollars.

The Cook Collection is especially noteworthy for its balance. It contains not only the more dramatic garments and weapons usually preserved but also the mundane tools and implements necessary for the life of a hunter-warrior. Many of the articles are linked to historic persons or events.

One may wonder how a rancher with little formal schooling came to make a collection of such quality and to preserve it so faithfully one hundred years ago. His efforts are especially remarkable, isolated as he was and without special funding. To find answers, we must turn to the story of the rancher himself and consider his natural traits.

James Cook, son of a British sea captain, was born in Kalamazoo, Michigan, in 1857. His father commanded a ship on the Great Lakes at the time and had settled in Michigan.

While still very young, James learned to handle a gun in the woods around his home and picked up other skills which later proved useful to him as a scout. James dreamed of going to the West. Like many another boy of that day, he had been fascinated from childhood by the many tales he heard of the frontier.

Motherless, with their father usually away on the ship, James Cook and his brother, Jack, lived in separate foster homes paid for by their father. They learned to fend for themselves without parents to take their part. Schooling was brief. James Cook said that a school "year," back then, lasted only until money that had been accumulated to pay a teacher ran out. Some "years,"

therefore, lasted about three months.

Fortunately for Jim, his foster mother was a former teacher. She required him to learn everything taught at the school. He was, thus, better equipped to continue with self-education than might have been supposed after only three years of grade school. In 1866, at the age of nine, James left his foster home and went to work on his own. He apprenticed first for two years in a machine shop. Next he tried his luck as a cabin boy with a ship on Lake Michigan, but that lasted only as far as Chicago. He subsequently boarded a steamboat and headed for Kansas, arriving in Leavenworth.

In Kansas, he fell in with cowboys who had just brought a big herd of cattle up the trail from Texas. In their company, he was soon on his way to San Antonio, where, not yet in his teens, he was hired as a cowboy on Ben Slaughter's ranch in the brush

country. His companions were mostly Mexican vaqueros. Cook said later that he never saw another young white boy his age in those old cow camps.

Jim's life was filled with hardship and danger, but it suited him. He was soon known for marksmanship and fearlessness. With other "brush poppers," he gathered longhorn cattle, "wild as deer," weathered stampedes and skirmishes with Comanches, having horses shot out from under him and taking an arrow in the leg. Several times in the 1870s, along with other cowboys, he trailed large herds of cattle from Texas to the northern plains. He took his turn singing to the bedded-down herd at night and sleeping out "Texas-style," (defined as "lying on your stomach and covering it with your back"), and meeting hazards as they came with the required hardihood.

Cook learned Spanish from the vaqueros he worked with. He picked up Indian sign language from the famed frontiersman, Jim Bridger, on an early trail drive. Thereafter, encountering Indians on the northern plains, he was able to begin communicating with them. Next he started learning Sioux. His grasp of the tongue, on more than one occasion, spared him and his trail companions unpleasant surprises. Cook's eagerness to learn what he could of their language and customs endeared him to the Sioux.

Cook was known as one of the best marksmen of his time and place. On trail drives, he was the individual designated to secure game for the crew, his Winchester carbine always carried in the chuck wagon. All the while, Cook entertained a dream of becoming a full-time big game hunter.

After years of cattle drives in the 1870s, Cook realized his dream. In 1878, having just completed a trail drive, he went to Cheyenne, Wyoming, and set out at once on his new career. Soon he and his partners were selling game to the railroad and guiding parties of wealthy hunters on expeditions, using Cheyenne as a base. During those years, he also guided such scientists as the paleontologists O.C. Marsh and E.D. Cope, Yellowstone explorer F.V. Hayden, and Clarence King, the first head of the U.S. Geological Survey.

In late autumn of 1878, the same year Cook established himself in Cheyenne, Dr. Elisha B. Graham, a New York physician, moved his family to Cheyenne. Cook soon met the Grahams. Little did he know at the time that their young daughter, Kate, would prove to be the love of his life.

By the spring of 1879, Dr. Graham had started a ranch on the Niobrara River in Nebraska some 100 miles northeast of Cheyenne. Graham was helped in choosing this location by a friend, "Portugee" Phillips. Phillips was famous in the West for his heroic ride in 1866, from Fort Phil Kearney in northern Wyoming to Fort Laramie in the south, through a blizzard in the dead of winter. It had been a desperate effort to aid Fort Phil Kearney after Fetterman and his troops had been wiped out there, leaving the fort all but defenseless. After Phillips guided Dr. Graham to the spot that was planned as headquarters for the new ranch, Graham bought a herd of cattle and placed the animals under the care of a foreman. He also had two log houses and other structures built. Thereafter, the Grahams vacationed each summer at the ranch. They called it the 0 4 Ranch because it was near the 104th meridian. Soon James Cook was visiting them there each summer.

In 1882, while he was a professional hunter, Cook was asked by British sportsmen to help establish ranches for them in New Mexico. These were men he had taken on hunting trips. In their company, he went to the south-western part of New Mexico and founded the W S and S U Ranches. These enterprises were in the heart of Apache country, at a time when the Apache wars were at their height. For the next five years, Cook ran the W S Ranch while helping the Army fight Apaches. He served as a scout, particularly during the Geronimo campaign.

During the years Cook was in New Mexico, the paleontologist E.D. Cope was his guest for several weeks at the W S Ranch. Cope told Cook much about the significance of fossils in tracing the earth's history, information which he absorbed with enthusiasm. Cope and O.C. Marsh, of Yale, were the two leading paleontologists on this continent at that time. Although famed for antagonism toward each other, it happened that, separately, they opened Cook's eyes to the world of fossils. The subject interested him for his entire life.

In 1884, while on one of his summer visits to the Grahams at their 0 4 Ranch, Cook and Kate found fossil bones while they were out riding. These were the first fossils collected at what later became famous as the Agate Fossil Quarries. Based on what he had learned about fossils from scientists he had guided, Cook saw that this find could be important. Some time later, after he and Kate had married and purchased the 0 4 Ranch, he alerted scientists to the presence of the fossils. As a result, the quarries were discovered much earlier than they would otherwise have been.

In 1886, Cook left New Mexico and returned to Cheyenne to marry Kate Graham. By then he was 29 and Kate was 18. He took her back to the W S Ranch in New Mexico where they prepared to make their home. However, after a year with Apache raids occurring all around them, and with Kate expecting their first child, they decided to return to Cheyenne. Harold Cook was born there in 1887. Shortly thereafter, the young family moved to the 0 4 Ranch on the Niobrara River in Nebraska and settled there, renaming it Agate Springs Ranch. Eleven years later, in 1898, the Cook's only other child was born in the Post Surgeon's house at Fort Robinson, Nebraska. John Graham Cook grew up strong and capable, only to die in the flu epidemic of 1918.

In 1904, O.A. Peterson of the Carnegie Museum in Pittsburgh opened the first quarry at the Agate site. The next year, E.H. Barbour of the University of Nebraska came to Agate. Then, in 1906, Albert Thomson of the American Museum of Natural History

in New York arrived to collect fossils. Subsequently, year by year, parties came from the Field Museum in Chicago, the Colorado Museum in Denver, and from Yale, Harvard, Princeton, and many other institutions. All were made welcome by James Cook, who hoped that extensive work would be done in the quarries during his lifetime so that he could know of the results.

Harold Cook, the son of James and Kate, developed a boundless enthusiasm for paleontology while he was growing up on the ranch and his interest in fossils endured throughout his life. Harold spent time in the fossil quarries with the experts who came to Agate and learned all he could from them. When the time came for him to go to university, he studied under Dr. E.H. Barbour at the University of Nebraska. Harold then went to Columbia University in New York and, while there, worked in the paleontology laboratory of the American Museum. In 1910, he married Dr. Barbour's daughter, Eleanor. As newlyweds, they homesteaded the section of land that included the fossil quarries, on which he had filed a claim in 1908 when he turned 21. Their homestead cabin, later used extensively by fossil collectors, came to be known as East Agate or, simply, the Bone Cabin. Thus it happened that summers at the ranch

were enlivened not only by Indian visitors but also by numerous scientists who worked and observed at the fossil quarries.

James H. Cook is shown in his buckskin hunting suit. Photo taken in 1886 when Cook was 29 years old. He is holding the Winchester 22 rifle that he used for trick shooting and competitions in several states.

After James and Kate bought the ranch in 1887, James soon invited his Indian friends to visit there. From that first year onward, Sioux and Cheyenne leaders came with their families, pitching their tipis on the banks of the Niobrara, hunting pronghorns with Cook, and talking for long hours. Listening to their tales of war and the hunt, he tried to visualize what their lives had been like when the bison were plentiful, before the white men came.

James Cook's son, Harold, later wrote of those early visits:

A great many of the older Indians came here to visit when I was a boy. Once, I recall, more than fifty wagons pulled in. As they were always short of food, that made a practical problem for us. The first big bunch I can remember who came and camped here were Cheyennes, many of whom had been in that famous fighting, when they fought their way back

from Oklahoma where they had been taken as prisoners. Photographs were taken of that camp, when I was about three years old (1890). It was common for anywhere from three or four to a dozen or twenty wagon loads of Indians to visit and counsel with my father. (1)

Red Cloud came to the ranch many times with his family. It made a hard trip for the old warrior, traveling from the Pine Ridge Reservation in South Dakota for several days in a springless wagon box. Still, he and the other elders wished to come as long as they were able. Red Cloud's last visit to Agate was recorded in a letter written May 10, 1908, by Kate Graham Cook to her sister Clara.

Well, old Red Cloud is here. Nineteen teepees came on Wednesday last. It was a sight to see the wagons and horsebackers come stringing down the hill road, singing their song about "Wambli

Cigala" [the Sioux name for James Cook] as of yore.

Old Red Cloud was able to get out of his wagon with little help, which surprised me. But when he was seated on the ground, his sightless eyes facing the western sun and his trembling hands trying to tighten his blanket about him it could be seen how feeble he was.

Jack Red Cloud (the "Red Cloud" who is exhibited in the shows) stooped over him and shouted our names as we took his hand. His face expressed great emotion, and his voice, as he greeted us. It was very pathetic to me.

Yesterday I went alone to his teepee where Jack Red Cloud's wife and Philip Romero's wife sat with him doing bead work. Romero's wife was a Carlysle girl and Maggy, her daughter, worked one summer for me you may remember. Well, they roused Red Cloud up – he sleeps most of the time – and I gave him a heavy blanket to rest on, as I had seen his bed was very hard. Then with Mrs. Jack shouting in his ear, I talked to Mrs. Romero and she translated to Mrs. Red Cloud, and she to him.

First I told him how glad I was to have the great head chief of the Sioux nation come to see us. His face lit up pleasantly and he replied that he wanted to come once more, and then he was ready to die. I asked him how he felt about going, and he said he had always had a brave heart in life, and he was not afraid to die. He said he was so nearly dead now that he often saw his wife, father and mother and talked with them.

Then they told me often when they would talk among themselves he would call out to them to keep still as he wanted to hear what his wife or father or mother were saying to him.

The Indians have brought us many things of historic value — wooden bowls, "great horn spoons," pincers for plucking beards and eyebrows, and a real scalp of a Mandan Indian taken by an Indian named White Whirlwind.

We have killed beef for them, and given them vegetables and other things, and they gave a dance night before last in the willows by a big camp fire. Many new neighbors came to see it with their children.

Jack Red Cloud came for me, so I did the squaw dance with him around the fire. Even Mother and Mrs. Bassett (the missionary) and Jack and Jim were led out, although they did not last long. One old squaw with a shrill treble voice took Jim with measured tread three times around the fire to the music of the tom-tom and the chosen singers. (2)

Less than a year later, Red Cloud was dead. During this same time, Kate, at the age of 41, suffered a mental breakdown and was hospitalized for the rest of her long life. Coming to terms with her fate was so difficult for her husband and son that they never again could speak her name without pain.

Throughout this time, the Indian families continued their annual visits, and they never came empty-handed. They brought old-time possessions no longer in use but with great meaning for them, as well as presents they had made for each member of the Cook family. Gifts ranged broadly, from small objects to large, ancient to new. From time to time, several horses, for example, were brought as gifts to the family at Agate. Hezé was a buckskin with typical mustang markings, Bat was the gift of Little Bat Garnier, and Billy American Horse was presented by American Horse, the great Sioux warrior and orator. It was Billy that James Cook chose to drive in his later years, to get around the ranch in a light buggy, after riding became painful for him.

There were also two full-sized gift tipis that Indian friends set up opposite the house. One year they brought a special half-sized tipi they had made for the enjoyment of the Cook grandchildren. Thereafter for years, Indian friends set up three tipis for the family each summer.

Smaller gifts included guns and knives, bags, ornaments, tools, and exquisitely-fashioned buckskin garments that had cost someone countless hours to make. Cook hung these in places of honor on the walls of his den and a nearby enclosed porch.

Another account of visits by Indian friends appears in a letter which Eleanor Cook, James Cook's daughter-in-law, wrote to her parents in 1914. The occasion was the 16th birthday of James and Kate Cook's son John.

About nine in the morning I looked out the window and saw a long string of wagons coming down through the pass. Harold and John had started to round up the herd in that direction. They rode on up the hill, since the wagons were easily recognized as those of our Indian friends from Pine Ridge, whom we have been expecting for a month or more.

Woman's Dress was in the lead, and much delighted to see them. "Huh, huh, heeeeiaa" he called as soon as they came within hailing distance, and then "Hallo,

Each summer, Indian visitors to Agate set up two large tipis and a smaller one for the children. The tipis were erected on the ranch house lawn, next to the sleeping house. Photo taken in 1924.

Sioux Indian camp at Agate about 1900. Now part of Agate Fossil Beds National Monument, this area is known as the Red Cloud Camp Ground Site. Grove of trees in background surrounds the ranch house.

my boyee!" He has been here more than others recently and he is my favorite, he is so jolly.

Woman's Dress has been eager to get an eagle for a long time. The first thing he asked Harold was whether or not he had one. When told that we do, he immediately asked that it be given to him. So, Harold and I went up and opened my moth proof feather-bag and got enough for a good showing all around. They were overjoyed to have them. I imagine that some of the gifts we receive next year will be decorated with eagle feathers. Certain of the feathers are sacred to them; and they are always glad to get any to use.

Soon they came over to the house with their gifts: a pair of moccasins for each one in the family, little girls included, several decorated war clubs, an "old-time" chokecherry grinder, several "what-is-its" and two unique bags. One is made of skin from the head of a buffalo calf, with eyes and ears done in beads. I wonder how long they must have had that as buffalo calves are not so numerous now. The second bag was made of a pronghorn fawn skin with the tail on, and tanned as only the Indians can tan such things. It is beautiful.

They are a fine-looking and well dressed group. One man, Left Hand Bear, is the handsomest Indian I ever saw in my life; very bright and nice.

Woman's Dress himself is sixty-seven years old. He has learned to speak English wonderfully since the last time I saw him, and he is glad to talk. His two grown sons came with him. It is Ed Woman's Dress whose baby is buried in the grove on the other side of the pond behind the house.

Arthur Woman's Dress is a handsome young fellow with the highest hat and the fanciest boots and the most brass-studded spurs I ever saw. He can live only a few months longer, I am afraid, as he is in the last stages of consumption. His little sister, who gave me the belt she wore to dance in, has died recently, and Ed has had two wives each of whom has died from the same cause. It is surely a dreadful scourge among them.

Arthur asked me if I would sew a dress for his mother. The next morning when I was sitting sewing in the enclosed porch, she came over. She had an old cloth under her arm, and in that a paper package containing two neatly basted white silk handkerchiefs for her boys, and a black velvet dress. It was cut like Mrs. Red Cloud's dress that we have in the collection; all very plain, with sleeves and dress in one, somewhat like the peasant styles we have worn, but still more simple. It was the first time I ever stitched a dress that was entirely basted, even to the hem; and it was none too easy to get into all the corners.

James Cook and Woman's Dress are shown with two historic rifles. Photo taken in 1913 by U.G. Cornell.

Cook is holding his Sharps 40-90 rifle, a gun he used for hunting as well as earning thousands of dollars in shooting competitions. The rifle was also used in a campaign against Geronimo's Apaches in New Mexico.

Woman's Dress is holding one of several guns which were concealed by Cheyenne women and used in their escape from Fort Robinson in 1879.

In the evening we invited the men over from the bunkhouse and all the Indians, for John's party. With seven in the family, and Bertha, who has been helping me lately, it gave us quite a number. Some of the Indians did not come because they can hardly see; and we planned to show pictures with the lantern.

After the pictures, we set off those explosive fruits. It was great fun to see the Indian women cover their heads with the blankets when the fireworks began to stream toward the ceiling, and then give a little scream when the fruit finally exploded and sent butterflies and birds around the room. Bertha and I scrambled around and fastened the cockleburs that are on each, to their blankets. They were much pleased, and chattered away at a great rate.

Then we pulled the table out into the center of the room, and their eyes simply bulged. It had the cluny lace table cloth on it, and every silver dish and candle stick and vase that we owned, and every flower, from pansy to loco. The cake was a hollow square, iced with white, and decorated with pink gelatin daisies and green angelica leaves, with John's age, initials and other statistics. It also had 16 pink rose candle holders, with pink candles.

John's grandmother, Mrs. Graham, poured the coffee, and Bertha the

chocolate. Bertha saw one Indian had none, so she passed him a cup of chocolate. He took a taste, and his look of horror was most amusing. We substituted coffee as soon as possible; but it was easy to see that he knew himself poisoned then and there. The crystallized ginger was another thing that surprised them a good deal, but they seemed to take to it kindly after the first shock was over. When we passed the mottoes they did not know what they had, so we went around helping them to snap them. How eagerly they seized upon the pins and beads that were inside! Imagine the most dignified middle-aged Indian that you ever saw, and then picture him with a pink tissue paper cap with long white streamers on his long hair. We all laughed until we were weak.

It was funny enough then, but after a while they decided to sing for John, and then it was too ridiculous to describe. They shut their eyes tightly and leaned back and opened their mouths as widely as possible, and then those caps, to add to it all! I do love to hear them sing. It all sounds better out of doors, anyway; and then I enjoy it more than anything else.

The cake had all sorts of fortune telling favors in it, and the Indians got several, but it was impossible to tell them what the idea was, as they do not tell fortunes. If "Wambli Cigala" (Little Eagle, their name for Father Cook) kills

a beef for them, that is fortune enough; and they do not care to hear about "going on a journey."

I thought as I listened to the Indians singing how few boys would celebrate their birthdays with their Indian friends. It did seem most fortunate that they had arrived in time. Woman's Dress stayed over today, and went with Harold and John to the Princeton camp, where they are working at the fossil quarries. The rest of the Indians left this morning. I hated to see them go, as I never enjoyed a visit from them so much before. (3)

Harold Cook, who grew up to be a geologist and paleontologist, created a "bone room" in his adjoining den to display specimens he collected. Both the Indian artifacts and the fossils excited interest among persons who came to the ranch on business. Soon word got around about the growing collections, and visitors began coming to the ranch expressly to see them.

From the first, James and Harold Cook shared their collections freely with the public. They believed that greater familiarity with Indian culture would bring more understanding of Indians as people. Both men were greatly interested in expanding public knowledge about fossils as well, particularly those from the Agate fossil quarries. They saw this sharing as essentially educational, something they enjoyed doing as a public service. Late in life, James Cook finally agreed to charge visitors a small admission fee; but, for many years, a guided tour through the Cook Collection was free.

James Cook was my grandfather, Harold my father. What I know about the Cook Collection of Indian artifacts I learned from them as I listened, on innumerable occasions from childhood to adulthood, as they described for visitors the history and meaning of these objects. Until the age of nine, I lived with my parents, sisters, and grandfather in the ranch house that was partly a museum. Three connecting rooms in the house were devoted to the collections. From those rooms, an open doorway led to the rest of the house. That doorway was tactfully hung with a curtain of slim brown bamboo beads to indicate where public access ceased.

From the outset, the numbers of people coming to see the museum at Agate increased steadily. By 1910, visitors had begun to arrive in droves. Soon it became impossible for James Cook to talk personally with every group of visitors that came, so family members pitched in to help. Harold Cook played a vital role in this regard, as did his wife, Eleanor, after they married in 1910.

As the second decade of the century passed and their children grew old enough, even the children were pressed into service to take people through the collections. From the age of six or seven on, my sisters and I were each assigned, in turn, the responsibility for conducting groups of adult visitors through the museum. We explained the artifacts in the same terms as did our elders, told the stories that went with them, and answered questions. Only occasionally did we need to refer for an answer to an adult family member.

Often, each of the three museum rooms had a separate group of visitors at one time, each with a different family member in charge. This continued, with changing groups, all day long. For the children, no better way could have been found to learn about the collections. There were no tape recorders in James Cook's lifetime. What our memories recorded comes closer than any other means available to giving an idea of what it was like to visit the Cook Collection when James Cook presided over it.

Upon entering the museum, visitors immediately saw hanging on the wall two pictographs painted on buffalo hide. Overhead, a large hide painting of the Custer battle at the Little Bighorn next claimed their attention. High on that same wall hung several Indian

saddles made of bone, wood, and rawhide, with bridles of various kinds. One was a hackamore of thick, unbraided hide stained red. It had just one rein with a loop at the end. The Sioux used this as a bridle, looping the end around the lower jaw of the horse.

Beyond these items were elaborate feather headdresses and a travois. On the floor, painted rawhide trunks and boxes were found. Above them were a ghost shield, flanked by bows and arrows, and a fringed and painted muslin ghost shirt from the time of Wounded Knee. A ceiling beam was hung with long guns from the war of 1812 and the Civil War. Beyond these were several pieces of varied historic interest such as an embossed powder horn, a bear trap, Indian stone grinders, and wooden butter bowls.

Harold Cook had collected the wealth of mineral specimens and fossils displayed in the Bone Room, which visitors entered next. This room, dedicated to paleontology, allowed visitors to examine materials from the Agate fossil quarries. There were, for example, skulls of the most numerous animal found at Agate, the little rhinoceros. It had two horns perched side by side on the end of the nose, not tandem as in today's rhinos. Its scientific name is *Diceratherium cooki*. The genus name, *Diceratherium,* means "two-horned beast," while the species name, *cooki,* honors James Cook, the man who introduced scientists to the fossil deposit. Another Agate fossil represented there was the tooth of the giant hog, *Dinohyus* (terrible hog), that stood six feet high at the shoulder. One of the most interesting Agate fossils in the exhibit was a leg of *Moropus,* a long-extinct, strange creature that resembled a draft horse with over-long neck, sloping hips, and grotesque claw-like hooves.

The Bone Room held a variety of fossils – skulls, jaws, and limb bones – that Harold Cook had collected on his field trips. Since the horses and camels that were native to the area had long been extinct in North America, it was not surprising that most visitors to the Cook ranch were amazed to learn that North America was the cradle of the race for such familiar animals. They exist today only because they migrated to other continents and survived there. That Nebraska had at one time harbored many different three-toed horses and a rich array of camels, rhinoceroses, and elephants was an idea that most visitors had never encountered.

In the Bone Room, a skull of the giant rhinoceros-like Titanothere lay on a table top, still partly encased in its plaster field cast. It almost gave substance to the Sioux legend about a Thunder Horse that plunged down in storms to wreak havoc. Modern skulls of coyote, wolf, horse, pronghorn, and bison were also present, as was an ancient, though not fossil, human skull from near Vancouver, British Columbia. This human skull generated particular interest because of the stone arrow point half-buried in it. "You can tell what he had on *his* mind," was the crisp comment made by our mother, Eleanor B. Cook, when she escorted people through this room. The saber-toothed tiger skull from the Rancho la Brea in California excited much comment, as did the mounted head of a grey wolf that James Cook had shot from the front door of the log house in the early 1890s.

Visitors often asked how it was possible to tell what animal a given fossil was. We explained that certain characteristics hold true through all the dogs, or all the camels, whether ancient or modern, especially in the teeth. Thus, a person familiar with deer teeth can recognize teeth from another deer, fossil or not. When asked how he knew a certain tooth was that of a horse, for example, James Cook would pick up a modern horse tooth together with one from a fossil horse. Holding them so the similarity could be seen, he would speak in the following words:

There is nothing in the world with a tooth like a horse, but a horse; or a cow, but a cow; or the dog or the cat or the human family. They are all distinct from one another, as a living horse is distinct from a cow.

Visitors next paused in a tiny hall often referred to as "the curio corner." Odds and ends accumulated there, including a ship in a bottle which had been assembled in prison by a former ranch hand. Also found were dried specimens which included a millipede, a scorpion, and a tarantula such as James Cook had encountered in his Texas cowboy years. He dubbed these "Faith, Hope and Charity," to the amusement of visitors. Finally there was a large tray filled with flint projectile points picked up at Agate over the years, a reminder of the peoples who lived here during prehistoric times.

Moving through another doorway, under a festoon of rattlesnake rattles strung on thread (all killed at Agate), visitors entered the Indian Room, as James Cook's den was known. There the bulk of the Indian collection was on display. The walls were laden with splendid skin garments, bags, moccasins, peace pipes, and war clubs – both ceremonial and strictly-business – and the human scalps that some of them had collected. Other items on display included beautiful, beaded and quilled "heart bags" for pipes and smoking materials, and a Sun Dance whistle made from the long, hollow bone of an eagle's wing. (4) Also included were hairbrushes made of stiffened porcupine tails, wooden flutes, and an otter skin quiver full of arrows.

Hung in a place of honor in the Indian Room was the original portrait of Chief Red Cloud that had been painted from life in this same room in 1902. Beneath it was the shirt he had worn and the single eagle feather (indicating a chief) he wore in his hair that day. A small, wood-framed mirror that Red Cloud had carried in his youth was also on display here.

Another historically significant item was the whetstone and its worn leather sheath that Crazy Horse was carrying when he died. It was later given to James Cook by the sister of Crazy Horse.

The Indian Room housed several guns that had special meaning for Cook. First, there was the old Sharps carbine, decorated with brass tacks, that Little Chief had given him. This gun had been used in the Custer fight in 1876 and again at Fort Robinson in 1879 when warriors of Dull Knife's band held off the soldiers long enough for women and children to escape. (5)

These people were Northern Cheyennes who had fought their way back from Oklahoma where they had been taken as prisoners and where many had died. Although the Army thought the Indians were disarmed when they were captured in the Nebraska sandhills and put under guard at Fort Robinson, the Cheyenne women had managed to keep eight rifles. They had taken the guns apart and concealed them under their clothing or under the coals of camp fires. James Cook often pointed out that the stock of this gun carried deep scars caused by burns it sustained while buried under a fire.

Nearby in the same room was the Sharps 40-90 that Cook had used in hunting big game and, later, depended on in the Geronimo campaign. With this gun, Cook made an unusual shot about 1880, which he described as follows:

After leaving Cheyenne with a party of English sportsmen, which included Mr. Harold Wilson, we camped for luncheon. While eating luncheon this antelope came on a hill quite a distance away and snorted at us. Some members of the party of British sportsmen who had hunted in various parts of the world wanted me to shoot at him with my Sharps rifle.

I told them the distance was too great

for any rifle, but they insisted, so I took my Sharps 40-90 and rest stick, sat down and took as careful aim as I could over the highest sights I could raise, and to my surprise the antelope fell dead, the bullet striking him square in the center of the chest.

Members of the party, who had hunted with the Boers' most noted trackers and shots in Africa, jumped to their feet and yelled, "That's the best shot I ever saw!" and two of them stepped the distance to where the antelope fell, the distance being 1,400 steps. About 1,400 yards. Wilson talked so much about that shot that his sister painted the head on ivory and brought it to me, about 1882. Wilson took the head to England and it was kept in the hall at Oxford college for quite a long time. (6)

Once settled on the ranch at Agate, James Cook read widely, particularly anything he could find related to the old West. He was dismayed to see how little was authentic. In the popular press, mythologizing of the old West was already under way with a vengeance. Cook found it intolerable that the hard life of the frontier should be misrepresented for the sake of cheap romance. He could not accept the distortions propagated by writers who had never experienced the life they attempted to describe.

Glancing around James Cook's den (the Indian Room) in 1922, one begins to understand the scope of the Cook Collection and the generosity of Red Cloud and his tribal membership.

From left to right, beginning on page 16: The southeast corner, with its display of Indian clothing, moccasins, and ceremonial trappings.

The south wall of the den showing Red Cloud's portrait which was painted in this room.

Cook's desk in the northwest corner, with his safe being used to support a collection of firearms.

Many different kinds of fossils were displayed in the Bone Room of the Cook Museum at Agate. The rhinoceros skull is seen in the center, and the leg of Moropus is at right. Photo taken in 1922 by Albert Thomson.

By then, the time was long past when cowboys gathered wild cattle in the brush country of Texas and drove them hundreds of miles to the northern plains without encountering a single fence. The days when they lived on abundant game along the trail and faced the danger of stampedes and Indian attacks had all vanished. Cook saw that, if an accurate account of that experience were ever to be set down, someone who had been there would have to do it.

Cook had long polished the telling of his tales, speaking to the Nebraska State Historical Society and other groups as well as to people in his museum. Now he began to write. One by one, his articles appeared in magazines. As he wrote, family and friends provided help and encouragement. It was slow work, all in longhand, since he never learned to type. Finally, James Cook's first book, *Fifty Years on the Old Frontier,* was published in 1923. It became a classic of western literature and brought widespread recognition. Cook continued writing short pieces and historical notes as long as he lived. A second book, *Longhorn Cowboy,* was published shortly after his death in 1942. In 1960 he was selected, posthumously, as an honoree in the national Cowboy Hall of Fame.

A glance at the active career of this frontiersman gives the viewer little reason to anticipate that Cook would prove to be a natural historian, a conservator of Indian culture, or a writer in the making. Yet, in every age and place, each person's impact depends on his personal attributes. James Cook was gifted with keen intelligence, a talent for languages, a remarkable memory, and an insatiable desire to learn. He was open to new experiences, unhampered by class or racial stereotypes. Befriended as a boy in Texas by Mexican vaqueros, he valued their friendship and expertise and profited by learning their language and skills. Among the Sioux, he quickly saw the worth of the lives they had lived and were now forced to abandon. He began to understand their point of view and to grasp their tongue.

Asked in later years how he could be friendly with Sioux and Cheyenne who had made life hazardous for pioneers in this region, I heard him answer many times in words like those which follow.

These people smoked a pipe of peace with me; they were my friends. We understood each other. I was never an "Indian lover." Some Indians needed killing, just as some white men did. But among Indians there were great hunters and brave warriors whose leadership and fearlessness were recognized by officers in the U.S. Army who opposed them. When white men came and took their hunting grounds, they naturally fought to protect them. If I had happened to be born an Indian, I would have done the same. In fact, I strongly suspect that I would have been a very bad Indian, from the white point of view.

From this background flowed the events that led to creation of the Cook Collection. Without James Cook's combination of traits, his friendship with Indian leaders would never have developed, nor would Indians have brought the gifts that make up the collection. Today, through these artifacts, the public can enjoy an intimate glimpse of a culture now vanished. Yet, without the foresight of the people who brought gifts for safekeeping, and the foresight of the man who faithfully preserved them – and influenced his descendants to preserve them after him, there would be nothing to see today.

In the list below are the names of Indian friends who visited James Cook at Agate. They are listed in no particular order and do not by any means represent a complete list.

Red Cloud (Mahpiya-luta)
Young Man Afraid of His Horses
American Horse
Woman's Dress (called also One Soldier and Bob-Tailed Horse)

Baptiste Garnier, ("Little Bat")

Baptiste Pourier, ("Big Bat")

Little Wolf

Good Lance

Two Lance

Short Bull

He Dog

Frank Goings

Clear Sky

Red Bear

John Kills Above

Jack Kills Chief

Jack Red Cloud

Phillip Romero

Red Hawk

Little Hawk

Little Wound

Little Chief

Little Crow

Wolf's Ears

Red Head (Pahin Sha)

Left Hand Bear

Blue Shield

Chicken Hawk or Beaver's Heart

Calico

Standing Bear

Mini Lee Ha (also known as Minihuha)

Jumping Eagle

Bone Necklace

Good Cloud

Runs Above

Walking Bull

Red Cloud's daughter, Mrs. John Kills Above, with James Cook about 1934.

Clear Sky at Agate in 1915, wearing clothing he wore in the Wild West Show.

Left, John Kills Above (son-in-law of Red Cloud), with Jack Kills Chief at Agate about 1915.

This photograph was taken at the formal dedication of the Red Cloud Agency Monument near Fort Robinson, Nebraska, in 1932.

Pictured from left to right, are: John Kills Above, James H. Red Cloud, James H. Cook, Agnes Red Cloud, Laura Red Cloud and Mrs. John Kills Above (Susan Red Cloud).

Clear Sky and his family at Agate in 1922.
Photo by Jim Wilson.

Red Cloud
Chief of
Sioux Nations

Bessie Sandes Butler
1902

21

Chief Red Cloud's portrait, his shirt, and eagle feather are featured items in the Cook Collection. The portrait was painted by Bessie Sandes Butler in 1902 at Agate Springs Ranch.

These objects illustrate the artistic possibilities explored by the Sioux in decorating their possessions. Carved stone is shaped expertly in both the representation of a mountain sheep on the war club and in the eagle's claws clutching the pipe bowl. The gauntlets are beaded in the naturalistic type of design that Lalee Garnier employed, as opposed to the geometric motifs ordinarily used by the Sioux.

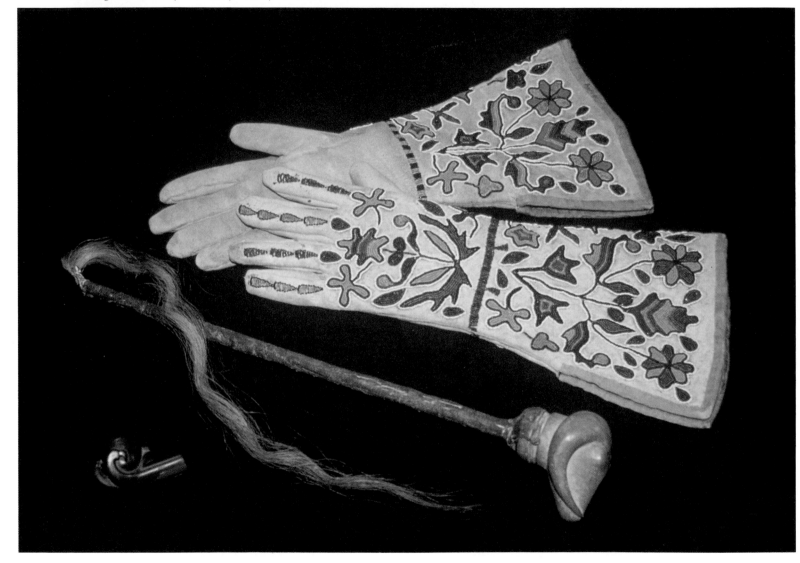

The Cook Collection contains more than 60 pairs of moccasins, most of which are elaborately decorated. At the center, top, are Red Cloud's ceremonial moccasins. This was always pointed out to visitors to the Cook Museum at Agate. Red Cloud's moccasins clearly had been worn, but the beaded soles are intact. The pair at the lower right, made for a youth, employs the turtle motif in the design of the soles. The child's pair at lower left was made for one of the Cook children. The pair of moccasins at upper right illustrates the use of quills and beads combined.

This striking pictograph was done on a cowhide at Agate, about 1898. It shows the Custer battle scene at the Little Bighorn in 1876. Among those who painted the hide were several Sioux who had fought at the Little Bighorn.

Hide Paintings

Pictographs painted on hide are an important aspect of the Cook Collection. One, on buffalo hide, records Red Cloud's name and lodge sign. It was painted by Jack Red Cloud in 1909, the year of the old chief's death. A second painting on buffalo hide describes a buffalo hunt. Tipis representing a camp are lined up at one end. Hunters are seen attacking the buffalo from slightly behind and to one side. Their method, they told James Cook, was to strike the animal behind the ribs so that the arrow went quartering forward, fatally damaging heart and lungs. In this pictograph, the buffalo is seen bleeding at the mouth, demonstrating that the hunt is a success.

A painting of the Custer battle, in Indian picture writing on a large cow hide, is one of the most striking objects in the collection. This extraordinary pictograph was made at Agate about 1898 by a group of Sioux men, many of whom had themselves fought in the battle of the Little Bighorn twenty-two years earlier. When that battle took place, James Cook was hunting nearby in Wyoming. After learning of the battle, he was one of the first people on the site. In later years, when Indian friends who were in that battle visited him, he questioned them closely about what happened there. Rather than explain it verbally, the Indians offered to make a picture of the battle if he would furnish an especially-prepared hide. When this was done and the hide staked out, several men assisted with the painting, using traditional pigments for the work.

Harold Cook, twelve years old at the time, remembered that Jack Red Cloud was one of the group who painted the battle scene. Unfortunately, he could not remember the names of other participants. Harold later wrote the following comments about that painting session.

The older men who "sat in" on painting the pictograph were greatly interested and they would often stop, consult, and discuss details, using vivid sign language, before one of them would proceed with the drawing. (7)

The painting shows uniformed soldiers on foot, mounted warriors attacking, and a large circle of tipis symbolizing the huge Indian encampment nearby. In one lower corner is the symbol for Red Cloud, and there are marginal symbols elsewhere for which the meanings have been lost. There is no doubt, however, as to the meaning or historical accuracy of a scene immortalized to the left of center, at the bottom.

There, a salmon-pink horse with long legs, obviously a tall cavalry horse, is shown in full flight from a group of Indians on the shorter-legged ponies of the Sioux. The uniformed rider has outdistanced the warriors and his safety seems assured; but, at that moment, he has turned his pistol toward his own head and killed himself. The incident made a big impression on the Indians, among whom suicide was unknown, Cook was told. Later it was learned that the suicide was a Lieutenant Doctor Lord who happened to ride with the troops into battle that day and presumably was crazed by what he had witnessed.

The Red Cloud Portrait

Among the most interesting and historically valuable objects in the collection is a large oil painting of Chief Red Cloud, the only portrait ever painted of him from life. He is shown in full ceremonial dress, with the single eagle feather of a Chief in his hair. His shirt of supple deerskin is fringed lavishly and decorated with wide bands of porcupine quillwork in purple and gold. The shirt and eagle feather were given to James Cook and are a part of the collection.

The manner in which the portrait came to be painted is a story in itself. Many times when they talked, Cook had suggested that Red Cloud should have his portrait painted. Cook pointed out to Red Cloud that he was an important figure in the history of the West and emphasized that if he did not have his portrait made, in time to come no one would remember what he looked like. Red Cloud, for his part, was reluctant to consent because among the Indians there was a belief that, if a person allowed his likeness to be made, he would thereby lose his strength.

Eventually, Cook's urgings prevailed. In the year 1902, one morning when Red Cloud was visiting at Agate, he appeared without warning at the door of the ranch house in full ceremonial garb, saying "I am ready to have my portrait painted." It is easy to imagine the consternation such an announcement would ordinarily have caused at the turn of the century on an isolated ranch – the explanations, and the regret over lost opportunity.

But, by great good fortune, a young woman artist chanced to be visiting at the ranch. A former classmate of James Cook's wife, Kate, her name was Bessie Sandes Butler. A graduate of the Chicago Art Institute, specializing in portraiture, she had brought paints and canvasses with her to the ranch. Thus, Red Cloud seated himself with great dignity in James Cook's study and the artist was summoned. She started work at once.

When completed, the painting hung for sixty years in the room where it was painted. Red Cloud is seen with an expression of stoic sorrow. Among those who knew him best, the portrait was considered an exact likeness. After his death in 1909, one old Sioux friend of his, seeing the portrait for the first time, screamed and, throwing her apron over her head, ran off into the hills above the valley. She had to be coaxed to return, certain she had seen his ghost.

According to old records, the artist later made a copy of her Red Cloud portrait. This happened when she had the unfinished painting at home with her in Michigan to complete. While she was working on it, a viewer was so impressed that he asked her to make a copy for him. This she did; therefore, it is possible that a copy of this original portrait, by the hand of the same artist, exists somewhere to this day.

War Shirts, Ghost Shirts

Ordinarily, in olden times, Sioux men went into battle nearly naked. Nevertheless, sometimes they reportedly wore their beautiful leather ceremonial shirts. James Cook was told that such a shirt was thought to protect the wearer from injury or death. The protection afforded was more metaphysical than actual, since buckskin is no barrier to an arrow, much less a bullet. But, because the Sioux held the most glorious death to be death in

Jack Red Cloud (left) and three other Sioux Indians are shown painting the Custer battle scene pictograph on a cowhide at Agate, about 1898.
(This same painting scene can be located in the lower left portion of the photograph of Agate Springs Ranch on page 3.)

battle, warriors may have dressed handsomely for that possible event. In time of peaceful conference or ceremony, on the other hand, to be a shirt-wearer was an honor reserved for leaders, James Cook was told.

Two leaders of the Sioux gave their ceremonial shirts to James Cook. One shirt, made of heavy buffalo hide stained yellow, came from American Horse, the great Sioux orator and warrior. It is ornamented with porcupine quillwork, reportedly made by a Cheyenne, in a vivid design of conventionalized flowers. A letter to Kate Cook from her mother, dated 1909, documents it as follows: "American Horse made a will, and willed Jim a suit and a war shirt. They are to bring it over when the grass gets good."

The other is Red Cloud's own ceremonial shirt. It is made of buckskin, soft as velvet. This splendid garment is decorated with two applied bands of solid quillwork in purple and gold about four inches wide. These bands extend over each shoulder and down to within a few inches of the bottom of the shirt, front and back. A triangular panel of quillwork, in matching design, ornaments the center of the neckline. The sleeves are finished with long fringe, each strip of which is exceedingly narrow and regular, made with exceptional skill. When she showed Red Cloud's ceremonial shirt to visitors, our mother often invited women in the group who had cut noodles to consider the difficulty of cutting these long, slim leather fringes so accurately.

A third shirt in the collection is muslin, stained, fringed, and lightly decorated. This is a ghost shirt, one used in the Ghost Dance craze that set the stage for the tragic massacre at Wounded Knee on December 29, 1890. Earlier in the month, James Cook had gone to Pine Ridge at the request of Indian leaders who hoped their friend might be able to assist in heading off the trouble they saw brewing. Help proved impossible in the prevailing atmosphere of misunderstanding and hysteria, and the tragedy of Wounded Knee followed. Many ghost shirts at that time were, like this one, made of whatever cotton fabric might be available, including flour sacks.

Good Road's Ceremonial Gown

The beautiful ceremonial gown in the collection belonged to Good Road, wife of Chief Red Cloud. It is ankle length, of the most velvety tanned doe elk skin, natural in color except for a band of smoke-tanned skin across the shoulders, upper yoke, and sleeves. The dress is of simple design, with the sleeves and bodice cut from one skin. Below the yoke, the gown hangs straight, finished with deep fringe at the hem and ends of the sleeves. Two bands of small beaded squares circle the dress in parallel, widely-spaced rows. From each square, two long, slender doeskin fringes hang.

The hem is decorated with a double band of beading above lavish fringe. A wide band of beading also edges the smoke-tanned yoke of the dress and extends to the ends of the sleeves. A parallel band of the same beading decorates the outsides of the sleeves from wrist to neckline and encircles the neck.

If Good Road's gown were made when she was young, it could easily date from the time of the Civil War or earlier.

In the accompanying photograph, the young woman shown wearing Good Road's gown is Agnes Gildea Thomson, the adopted daughter of Albert Thomson and his wife. It was Albert Thomson, of the American Museum of Natural History in New York, who collected in the Agate fossil quarries for more seasons than any other individual. His wife and Agnes often accompanied him when he worked at Agate. This photograph was taken about 1912.

Moccasins and Leggings

The Cook Collection includes many

Agnes Gildea Thomson is shown wearing Good Road's ceremonial gown. Photo taken at Agate about 1912.

Leggings were used largely for ceremonial purposes. This unusual pair, with moccasins attached, is decorated with beadwork which extends upward from the ankles.

pairs of moccasins, all beautifully decorated with beads, quillwork, or both. Two pairs belonged to Red Cloud. One of these was given to James Cook on May 12, 1908, on Red Cloud's last visit at Agate. It has signatures and the date written in ink on the soles. The finer pair, Red Cloud's ceremonial moccasins, were given by the old Chief to James Cook on a visit years earlier. These are elaborately beaded all over in multicolor on a white background, in perfect condition and exceptionally handsome. No doubt, when Red Cloud wore these, he was seated ceremonially and stepped on them lightly if at all.

There are two or three smaller pairs of moccasins that also are beaded all over, including the soles. Among these is an infant pair. These were Harold Cook's first shoes and thus date to his birth in 1887. Considering James Cook's friendship with Sioux and Cheyenne families, it is not surprising that his son's first baby shoes were moccasins made for him by an Indian friend. Harold's parents valued these baby moccasins too highly to use them except on "state" occasions. They soon carefully stuffed them to preserve the shape and then hung them in the collection.

There is a widespread idea that North American Indians beaded moccasins on the soles only for funerary purposes. Here, to the contrary, we have moccasins beaded on the soles for a new-born baby who lived to the age of 75. Here, also, we have ceremonial moccasins beaded on the soles and given to James Cook by the owner during the owner's long lifetime. Moccasins thus seem sometimes to have been beaded on the soles to honor a special person or a particular occasion. It is evident that the Sioux had no prejudice against beading moccasins on the soles other than practical considerations. It may well be that, for a person to have moccasins beaded on the soles, it depended more on the energy and devotion of women in his family than it did on custom.

Kate Cook's own moccasins were made by Yellow Bird, at Pine Ridge, in the early 1880s. During a visit to the Grahams at the 0 4 Ranch, James Cook heard Mrs. Graham and Kate express a wish to see an Indian reservation. Cook, accordingly, drove them to Pine Ridge and, while there, bought the moccasins for Kate. They are low-cut and slipper-like, without cuffs or ties, with beautiful floral beaded designs. They appear to have been worn very little, but, instead, to have been saved for the collection.

Three pairs of leggings are part of the collection. These were used largely for ceremony. One pair is trimmed with an extra-wide band of beading at the bottom, in geometric designs on a white background. This is handsome against the smoke-tanning of the deerskin. A second pair is also of supple, smoke-tanned deerskin. Here, each legging is fringed at the outer leg seam and trimmed with a narrow band of beading there and at the bottom. The third pair of leggings ends in an attached pair of moccasins. This pair is decorated with a narrow beaded band at the ankle that extends up the front.

Several pairs of child-size moccasins in the collection were given to Harold Cook's daughters, Margaret, Dorothy, Winifred, and Eleanor. Our grandfather, James Cook, immediately appropriated for the collection all the purses, moccasins, headbands, knives, strings of wampum, awls, sheaths, beaded bridles, dance war clubs, and other presents that were brought to us. As one of the granddaughters, I can attest that, among the gifts we individually received from Indian friends, the only objects exempt from this immediate appropriation were our play tipi and our ponies. Even as small children, we were given to understand the importance of preserving gifts from Indian friends and keeping them together. As it turned out, Grandfather modified slightly this disciplined approach late in his life. When his granddaughters came to visit during his last years, he sometimes picked out an object that had once been given to one of the little girls and returned it: perhaps a beaded leather bag, a pair of baby moccasins, or a doll.

Buckskin Hunting Suit

When James Cook became a big-game hunter in 1878, at the age of 21, he had a buckskin hunting suit made for himself. Beautifully tanned, soft, white skins were used. The shirt is tailored in a style similar to the cavalry officers' uniforms of that period, with a large, shaped front panel and brass buttons around the edges. The outer surface of each sleeve is decorated by a two-inch applied band fringed along both edges. The bands have quarter-inch holes punched at regular intervals and cloth in several bright colors placed behind the openings before the strips were sewn into place. This provides an attractive effect. Similar bands, with fringe, cut-outs, and colored inserts, decorate the trousers. Deep fringe ornaments the shirt back, below a decorated yoke.

This suit was made by Hank Clifford, an interpreter from Hitchcock County, who had married into the Sioux nation. Clifford ran the stage station about eighteen miles east of Agate where the Sidney-to-Deadwood trail crossed the Niobrara. Clifford and his wife made the suit, including areas of scrolled quilting, using a sewing machine screwed down to a plank, the wheel turned by hand.

After he lived at Agate, Cook wore the suit only on special occasions. Whenever his Sioux and Cheyenne friends did him the honor of visiting and dressing in their beautiful ceremonial garb, Cook responded by wearing this special suit. He was photographed wearing it many times while speaking sign language or counseling with groups of Indians on the lawn at Agate.

Two pairs of gauntlet gloves made for James Cook are in the collection. Each is beautifully decorated buckskin, one pair with beads and the other with quills. Whoever made one had not yet worked out the niceties of design; the thumbs are badly placed, making the gloves awkward to wear. (Our mother joked with visitors that the maker stood back and threw the thumbs at the gloves, sewing them on wherever they landed.) A third pair, youth-sized, solves this problem by attaching beaded gauntlet cuffs to commercial leather gloves. Also worthy of close inspection is the beautiful quillwork on a pair of buckskin arm protectors in the collection.

In 1896, when he was nine years old, Harold Cook received a beautiful buckskin suit from Short Bull, a nephew of Red Cloud. Short Bull was a renowned warrior who took part in the Custer battle and many other historic fights. He killed the animal from which the suit was made. His wife tanned the skin and made the suit, which consists of coat, trousers, and moccasins. Then, because she could no longer see to do beadwork, Mrs. Short Bull turned to the wife of Baptiste (Little Bat) Garnier for the beading. She worked the decorations before Short Bull and his wife brought it to Agate. (8)

The suit is expertly and lavishly beaded in handsome floral designs using both ordinary and cut beads that contrast nicely with the soft, white buckskin of the suit. The curving, naturalistic floral designs are in sharp contrast to the triangles, diamonds, and bars that dominate most Sioux design. Both Little Bat's wife and his sister, Lalee (Eulalia) Garnier, used these naturalistic designs in their expert beadwork. Lalee had been the wife of John Hunton, trader at Fort Laramie. Later, in the 1890s, she worked for the Cooks at Agate, and examples of her "beady work" are in the collection. James Cook thought it possible that her use of curving, floral designs was influenced by the

Dorothy Cook (left), Nancy Red Cloud, Margaret Cook, and Mary Red Bear are shown wearing buckskin children's clothing at Agate in 1916. Margaret Cook is wearing the little boy's suit made for her father, Harold, in 1896. That suit, also shown in the photograph at right, was a gift from Short Bull, one of Chief Red Cloud's nephews.

fact that Little Bat and Lalee were half French.

A smaller boy's suit in the collection was made in 1903 for Harold's young brother, John, when he was about five years old. His little suit, rubbed with yellow pigment, was sparely decorated with fringe and simple beaded bands at neck and cuffs. James Cook often remarked that the Sioux, like the British, placed great emphasis on the importance of the first-born son. This is evidenced by the comparative simplicity of the suit made for the younger son. Both boys wore the suits when Indian visitors came to Agate. Later, Harold's daughters wore these same suits for similar special events.

Belts and Ornaments

On ceremonial occasions, Sioux women often wore ornamental belts long enough to encircle the waist and hang to the hem of the gown. The belt that belonged to Good Road, wife of Chief Red Cloud, is made of dark buffalo hide, closely set with large, domed copper discs separated by nickel studs. James Cook was told that the discs had been beaten out of native copper, which no doubt was obtained through trade from Michigan. A second long belt in the collection is made of tan cowhide ornamented with beads and brass studs. It belonged to the daughter of Woman's Dress, the well-known Army scout. She wore it dancing until she became ill with tuberculosis. In 1913 she gave it to Eleanor B. Cook.

Although war and raiding were common events, much trading also took place. Through trade, Indian people obtained useful and ornamental materials and objects not otherwise available where they happened to live. An example of material freely traded was catlinite (pipestone) from Minnesota, a favorite for pipes and light war clubs.

Another example of trade goods found in the collection is a necklace of red seeds. The Texas Mountain Laurel *(Sophora secundiflora),* a large shrub, grows no closer to Sioux territory than the hill country in central Texas. (9) The seeds, which grow in a bean-like pod, are hard and poisonous, as the Indians well knew. Nevertheless, they made attractive beads of them. As it happens, when seeds fall to the ground, an insect drills into them and eats out the center. This leaves only the remaining side wall of the shell to be pierced to make a bead. Similarly, the Navajos today make beads of cedar berry seeds, aided by an insect that half-drills the seeds for them.

The scalp lock of a defeated enemy was an ornament and badge of honor for a warrior. When a scalp was removed from a victim, only a small patch of skin was cut away, not the entire scalp as has sometimes been supposed. Consequently, as James Cook liked to point out, victims of scalping who happened to be merely stunned, had been known to escape to live another day, with all but a full head of hair.

The small scalp piece, perhaps the size of a penny, was dried and wrapped to make a neat end. That scalp, tied with others, was then made into a bundle the size of which was determined by the prowess of the warrior. Young men who had not yet taken scalps in combat sometimes used false scalps of horsehair as stand-ins for the human scalps they expected to take in time. Both human scalp locks and their horsehair shams are included in the collection. Human scalps presented to James Cook were all donated by Red Cloud's old warriors, men like Blue Shield, Little Wound, and Young Man Afraid of His Horses.

Of all ornamental garb worn by Sioux and Cheyenne men, the great eagle feather headdresses were the most impressive. These were brought out for dances and special occasions and became, for most observers, the most characteristic part of the costume of the Plains Indians. Some headdresses used antelope horns as well as eagle feathers. One of these in the Cook

Collection was given to James Cook by Red Hawk of the Northern Cheyenne.

Headdresses usually had a beaded band above the eyebrows. Above this, the eagle feathers fanned out. The shaft of each feather was tightly bound for some inches and then sewed to the headband. Feathers were spaced correctly to insure maximum spread when the headdress was worn. At its tip, each feather had a downy "breath feather" attached or a few long horsehairs gracefully streaming.

From each side of the head, streamers were usually attached to the brow band. These were ten to twelve inches long and were made of mink skins, eagle feathers, ribbons, or whatever was available and attractive. Such a headdress commonly required at least two dozen eagle feathers. Many longer headdresses had a double row of feathers continuing down the back to the ankles of the wearer. The longer style of headdress required as many as eighty eagle feathers.

A string of charms in the collection was the gift of Little Chief. It was said to ward off bullets. The string is made of a leather strip on which are strung numerous tips of deer and antelope hooves and horns, plus seeds of the native plum, each on its own little thong.

A design in use among the Sioux and Cheyenne was the turtle. Cheyenne medicine men were known to predict the weather by use of a special "weather turtle." The turtle image appeared in beading and quillwork and occasionally as a stuffed object. James Cook was told that the turtle was a symbol of bravery to the Sioux. Close observers of nature, they knew that turtles are hard to kill. They had seen a turtle's heart, removed from its body, continue to beat for an hour or more in the hot sun. This meant to them that turtles have great courage and tenacity, qualities they wished to possess themselves. Therefore, Cook was told, the turtle designs they used on bags and garments symbolized the bravery of the owner. One pair of moccasins in the Cook Collection has a turtle design beaded on the soles.

Several beaded head bands in the collection are representative of those that women wore for dances. Beaded watch fobs, small deerskin purses, and beaded knife sheaths were other examples of articles worn according to the taste and desire of the owner.

Hairbrush and Mirror

Sioux women learned to make hair brushes out of porcupine tails at a time now lost to antiquity. The process was easy compared with many other tasks they performed. Porcupines were then, as today, fairly numerous and not difficult to find. With their slow gait and reliance on quills for defense, they were easy to catch.

Once having secured a tail, an Indian woman would cut a slit in it from end to end, and then remove the string of tail bones and any flesh. She then replaced the bone with whittled wood for stiffening, sometimes leaving a length of wood to project at one end for a handle. The skin was then sewed up around the wood and left to dry. An ornamental band of beads might be added, and possibly a sheath or a leather hanging thong. This made a brush of sorts, the best available. We often wondered how an Indian woman could possibly have used such a hairbrush, to which the answer had to be "with caution."

There is a small mirror in the collection, set in a crude wooden frame and badly scratched from long use. Red Cloud carried this mirror for many years, up until the time he was at Agate when Harold Cook was leaving for the University. Harold was to be gone for most of a year. Many of the Indians who gathered that day grieved at Harold's departure, remembering sons of their own who had gone away to school and never returned, having contracted white man's sicknesses. As the Indians lined up along the path to bid him goodbye, many were keening and

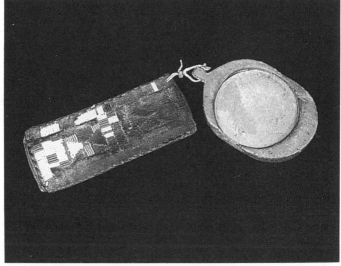

Far left: Sioux women made hairbrushes from porcupine tails. Those shown in this photograph are decorated with beadwork.

Red Cloud's personal mirror, shown at left, was given by the great chief to Harold Cook at the time he left Agate to attend university. A comb case is attached to the mirror.

Bottom: A string of charms given to James Cook by Little Chief consists of tips of horns and hooves of antelope and deer, as well as plum seeds.

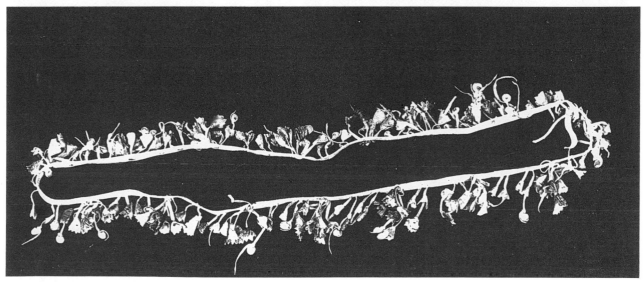

moaning. Then Red Cloud gave Harold this mirror, saying "You will have use for this – you are a young man. I am old, and no longer look in mirrors." (10) Since then, this little mirror has had an honored place in the collection.

Indian Tools

James Cook enjoyed pointing out to visitors that an Indian knife could always be recognized by the fact that it was sharpened on one side only. Whether this were a matter of custom or had further significance, he had not been told. Since an Indian had daily need of a knife, both as a tool and a weapon, it was kept handy in a sheath attached to the belt. Often he carried a whetstone as well, also in its own case. These sheaths and cases were often attractively decorated.

When James Cook first knew the Indians, he observed that a sharp knife was essential for their style of eating meat. To take a bite, an Indian would first grip a large piece in his teeth. Then, in one quick motion, he would slash off the piece he intended to chew, close to his lips, without ever cutting himself. This feat, matter-of-factly performed, never failed to excite astonishment in those who saw it done for the first time.

As hunters, Indians continually had need of good skinning knives; and, as warriors, they settled many hand-to-hand encounters with knives. It is therefore no surprise that the Cook Collection includes knives and whetstones as well as various sheaths to hold them.

James Cook had this to say about three of the knives in the collection:

Knife at the top (flag in sheath) is an old Hudson Bay knife, given to me by Calico. Scabbard goes with the knife. The knife in the beaded sheath is an old I. Wilson skinning knife that I brought from the battle of Wounded Knee. It is marked by the man who owned it. Was jabbed right down into the chest of a soldier. This is the kind of knife I used as a skinning knife when I was hunting. Just a 25 cent knife. I don't know that they are made any more. No scabbard with it.

The big knife alongside of it was given to me by Big-Foot Wallace of Texas and was used in the fight at the Alamo. The scabbard for it was made later as the old rawhide scabbard wore out. (11)

The reddish whetstone that Crazy Horse was carrying when he was killed at Fort Robinson in 1877 was given to James Cook by Crazy Horse's sister, the wife of Red Sack.

When Indians were hunting, tools such as hide scrapers and fleshers were much in use. Before iron was available to them, Indians used flint scrapers to remove flesh from inside the fresh hides. Later, fleshers were made of iron. Two such examples in the collection were made from rifle barrels, sawed off, flattened and notched like teeth at one end. The other end of each was bound with deerskin for a better grip and has a leather thong attached.

After a hide had been cleaned on the inside, an Indian would turn it over and use an elkhorn scraper to remove the hair from the outside. An elkhorn scraper was made of elk antler trimmed in such a manner as to provide a strong handle about nine inches long with a natural right-angle bend at one end. Indian women gripped these tools with both hands, placed the bent end firmly against the hide, and pulled back vigorously. An experienced woman could remove hair from a hide with complete success through vigorous use of this method.

In the Cook Collection, the older and darker of the two elkhorn scrapers belonged to Good Road, wife of Chief Red Cloud. Through years of heavy use, her hands alone wore clear through the smooth outer layer of antler, exposing the porous inner texture. Another style of scraper found in the collection was made from a branch of wood that grew in an almost perfect right angle to which an iron blade has been added. James Cook was told this tool was particularly useful for cleaning a fresh hide draped over a log.

Sioux and Cheyenne used many small stone hammers and pounders. Each had a rather short handle and a stone head that was flattened on one side. The stone head was covered with rawhide and was lashed to the wooden handle by rawhide thongs. Indians sometimes beaded these implements but often left them plain. Such a hammer was used primarily for crushing various fruits and berries for food. Wild currants, chokecherries, gooseberries, buffaloberries, and grapes, all native to the area, were dried and pounded, seeds and all, in a rawhide bowl. In making pemmican, the Indians placed boiled jerky in a rawhide bowl. They then pounded and mixed it with bits of fat and dried berries. Finally, the mixture was formed into small patties.

The Cook Collection has an example of an old buffalo hide bowl used for pounding up berries. A gift from Calico, the bowl was made from the skin of a buffalo's hump. It is a good-sized bowl, practical, lightweight, long-lasting, and easily carried when the owner moved camp.

A large stone mallet in the collection functioned like a sledge hammer. Its heavy stone head is securely bound to a strong handle covered with rawhide stitched into place. Among other uses,

this implement was used to break the cooked bones of buffalo, permitting the Indians access to that prized delicacy, the marrow.

Scoops, spoons, and dippers in the Cook Collection were made from the horns of buffalo and mountain sheep. Indians boiled such horns until soft and then cut and fashioned them into utensils while still hot. These were used daily in preparation and eating of meals.

Still another tool in frequent use was the bone awl, often made from the wing bone of an eagle. Awls were essential for punching small holes in leather. Through these, sinew from the ligaments of buffalo would be threaded. Thus, sinew was used in place of thread and awls in place of needles or punches. A good, sharp awl was valuable; hence it was kept for protection in its own slender case with flap cover to secure it. The case itself was often nicely beaded. One old awl, in a case decorated all over with beads in random colors, was given to James Cook by Mrs. Jack Red Cloud. She told him it was made at Fort Laramie in 1836, using as a base the big cord of a buffalo's neck, shrunk down when fresh. (12)

A special tool was used for straightening the bent or warped shaft of an arrow. For this, the Indians used the dorsal spine of one of the vertebrae in

the buffalo's hump. This yielded a flat bone about eight inches long, in which they made a hole at one end large enough for the arrow's shaft to fit loosely. The shaft was first soaked and its tip was then inserted in the hole. This bone device provided the necessary leverage so that a shaft could be bent repeatedly in a direction contrary to the warp as it dried, eventually straightening it. Such a tool in the Cook Collection was found by Harold Cook and Albert Thomson on a fossil-collecting expedition near Spoon Butte in 1908.

Shafts of arrows were sanded smooth by use of another device. It consisted of two rounded pieces of sandstone, each with a flat face that fit against the other. Between the flat faces were matching grooves, each about one-half the depth of an arrow's shaft. In use, the shaft would be placed in the grooves between the blocks. With the blocks gripped together in one hand, an Indian could use his other hand to run the arrow's shaft back and forth between the blocks to smooth it.

Porcupine Quill Work
Two special bags in the Cook Collection held porcupine quills, dyed and ready for use. One of these was the gift of Mrs. Jack Red Cloud. These bags were made of buffalo bladder. Although cracked and frail-looking today, buffalo

bladder is tough when new and, accordingly, worked well for holding quills. Plainly, no material easily punctured would be satisfactory for that purpose. As anyone knows who has ever handled quills, they are extraordinarily sharp at both ends. Worse yet, the "business end" is armed with tough barbs like the barbs on a fishhook, making extraction of a quill far more painful than the puncture itself.

The stunning designs worked out in porcupine quills by Sioux and Cheyenne women are a marvel on many levels. First there is the difficulty inherent in working with the quills themselves. Since it is almost impossible to handle quills carefully enough not to be stabbed by them, even to collect a supply risks painful punctures. Once gathered up, each quill had to be dyed, another tedious process involving having on hand a sufficient supply of native pigments. Quills were soaked in water for a short time before putting them in the dye.

For purple dye, they used fox grape. Red dye came from snakeberry root, buffalo berries, and squaw berries; yellow dye came from sunflowers and other sources. Finally, after a woman had enough dyed quills prepared, it was necessary for her to flatten each one for use. Some quill workers used a thumb nail; others would bite the quill between the front teeth and pull it through. Keeping tongue and lips out of harm's way at such a time must have been a neat trick. After all that, each quill was long enough for the equivalent of only two or three stitches at most.

Nevertheless, large and complex designs were worked on countless leather garments, using this difficult material. The skilled quill worker managed to tuck in both ends, leaving nothing to prick the wearer. Quills were often worked in a sort of flat braid immensely tedious to duplicate. Other than painting directly on hides, quillwork was the only means of surface decoration available to Indian women before they began to get beads in trade.

Tanning

Indians followed several steps in tanning hides. After the skin was removed from an animal, the first task was to scrape it thoroughly on the flesh side, leaving it clean. For some purposes, the hair was left on the other side. More often, hair would be scraped off with equal care before the job of tanning could begin. James Cook described to visitors the Indians' method of tanning in words such as these:

When a robe was to be made, one part of buffalo brains to two parts well-boiled liver was used, to which was added a little soft fat taken from the paunch of the buffalo. This material was spread over the inner surface of the hide, which was then carefully rolled up and firmly tied into a bundle. After being thus baled for about three days, the bale would be opened and the tanning material washed off the hide. When time allowed they would put a solution of brain and liver water on the flesh side of the skin three times, before starting the work of drying out and softening the hide.

Working the hide back and forth over a small rope made of the back sinews of buffalo stretched between two trees, or stakes set firmly in the ground, in time made the robe dry, soft and pliable. It was a most laborious process and required hours, plenty of muscle and no little skill to accomplish it. When an unusually good buffalo or elk skin robe was secured, it would often be decorated by pictographs, and sometimes with porcupine quills. (13)

James Cook often related that the Indians had told him they used two methods for tanning, one for white skins and the other for smoke-tanned skins. As he described it, "the last-named was thoroughly and repeatedly smoked during the tanning process, over an arch of willow sticks with a little fire underneath, the fire being made of materials that would produce a

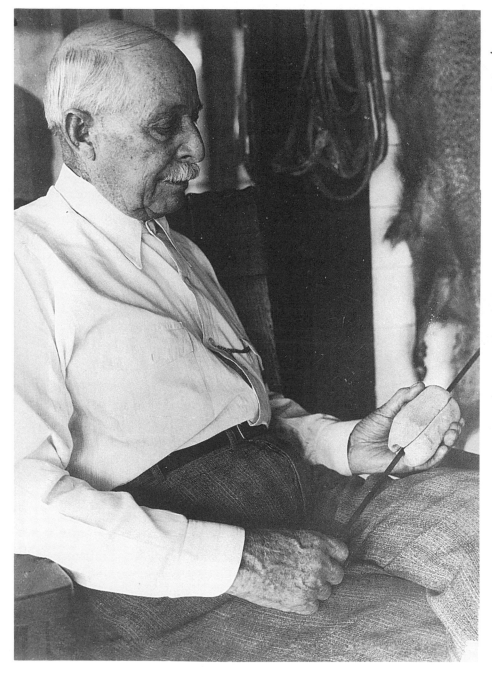

James Cook, in the museum at Agate in the late-1930s, is shown demonstrating how an arrow shaft was smoothed by drawing it back and forth between two pieces of sandstone.

Ladles or dippers were probably made from boiled and cut horn of buffalo or mountain sheep.

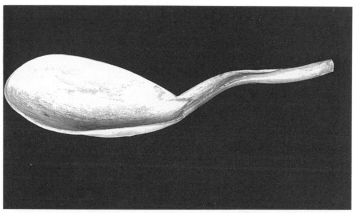

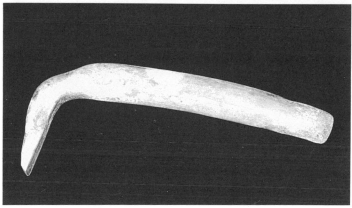

Hide scrapers, such as this one which belonged to Good Road (Red Cloud's wife), were usually made of elk antler.

heavy smoke and but little heat." (14)

Despite this demanding process, Indian women tanned hides so beautifully that many garments they made more than one hundred years ago are still supple and soft as velvet today.

Heart Bags and Pipes

Traditionally, an important possession of each warrior among the Sioux was his "heart bag." The heart bag held pipe and smoking materials, the use of which held great spiritual meaning for them. When a Sioux smoked the pipe, he was obligated never to speak "with a forked tongue" but always "from the heart." From this arose the term "heart bag," so James Cook was told. Sometimes the occasion for smoking was to make or confirm peace; from this arose the term "peace pipe" among white men.

Heart bags were not tobacco bags, as they have sometimes been described. James Cook pointed out that tobacco was unknown to the Sioux before white men came. The materials they smoked included the inner bark of the dogwood *(Cornus stolonifera),* dried buffalo chips, and various herbs. When the Sioux smoked the pipe, it was a serious and ceremonious affair that James Cook never tired of describing to visitors in words such as these:

Seating themselves in a circle, they filled the pipe and lighted it. Before smoking, they offered the pipe first to the Great Father above, pointing the stem upward. Then they offered it to the West, where the Great Spirit of Thunder presides; then to the North where the Spirit lives who sends the buffalo to the Indians; then to the East, where lives the Spirit of the Elk; then to the South, inviting the Spirit of the Sun to join them; and finally downward to the Mother of us all, the Earth. Then they smoked, passing the pipe around the circle to be smoked by each man present. (15)

Heart bags were generally long, flat, and fairly narrow, perhaps eight inches wide by twenty long. Often there was a drawstring thong at the upper end and several inches of fringe at the bottom. Decorations took many forms, employing beads or quillwork, or both. Heart bags included some of the most beautiful and varied pieces of craft work ever produced by the Sioux. Usually each side of a bag had a different design, each equally handsome. A bag presented to James Cook by the wife of Minihuha, for example, has a design in beads showing a mounted Sioux warrior on one side and a grazing elk on the other. Minihuha, who took part in the Custer battle, was one of Red Cloud's old warriors.

Some pipe bags were made of unusual materials. An example is the bag in the Cook Collection made of the whole skin of an antelope fawn with hair and tail left on. Two other unusual bags are made from the skin of calves heads, with eyes, ears, and noses beaded. The darker one is made from the head of a buffalo calf; the other a Hereford. All three of these exceptional bags were given to James Cook by Woman's Dress, the famous Scout with the U.S. Army. He had two other names – One Soldier and Bob-Tail Horse – but it was as Woman's Dress that he was known around Fort Robinson where he served the Army long and faithfully. (16)

Sioux pipes were expertly made, employing beautiful and interesting materials. The care lavished on their making was in direct proportion to the importance placed on the pipe-smoking ceremony in Sioux culture.

The oldest pipes used by the Sioux were made from tibia, or leg bone, of deer or antelope. One of these in the collection, in its own small leather sheath, was made for James Cook by Standing Bear. Subsequently, pipe bowls were made of a white stone the Sioux found "somewhere in the upper Mission River, before they got the catlinite hundreds of years ago," James Cook told visitors. (17)

The more recent pipestems in the collection were most commonly made

The pipe bag at left was a gift from Good Cloud. It is made of native tanned leather and has beadwork decoration. This same bag can be seen in the photograph of James Cook's den (on page 17), to the right of his desk.

Shown below is an awl case that is typical of several colorfully beaded cases in the Cook Collection.

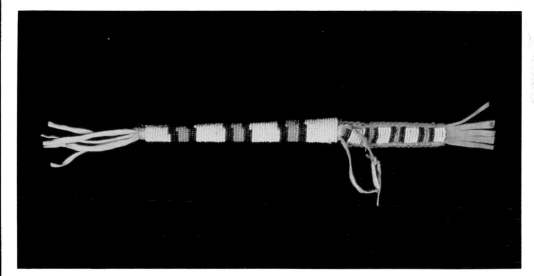

The Cook Collection contains a wide variety of small bags and pouches. This brightly colored grouping is representative. Beads, quills, or both, were used extensively for decoration.

This selection of nine pipe bowls from the Cook Collection illustrates the wide variety of styles and materials used. Catlinite, or pipestone, was the rock most commonly employed, but other stone was carved when it was particularly attractive. The buffalo head pipe bowl shown is one such example. Lead was sometimes used for decoration, as in the pipe bowl seen at upper right.

44

This colorful shield in the Cook Collection was probably used in ceremonial dances.

Parfleches were rawhide boxes or envelope-like pouches used to store goods. The trunk-like box shown here is typical of those which were painted with native pigments.

of wood, with handsome bowls carved of pipestone (catlinite). This material was acquired in trade with tribes who lived near where it originates, at the present site of Pipestone, Minnesota. Catlinite is a clay-like stone with enough iron in its composition to produce a strong rust color. It is fairly easy to carve and takes a nice polish. Pipes with bowls of this material were handsome and varied. In some, channels were cut to be filled with lead. Smoothed and polished, lead takes on a silvery look that the Indians found decorative. James Cook pointed out that heavy lead foil, such as then commonly lined packages of tea, worked easily for purposes like this and was used to enhance catlinite when available.

Pipestems of smooth wood were sometimes decorated with a wide band of quillwork near the mouthpiece and often further enhanced by wisps of dyed horsehair. One wooden pipestem in the collection is carved in a graceful spiral, divided by three rings, the whole then stained in bright colors. The catlinite bowl of this pipe is shaped to resemble the head of a tomahawk, for an altogether exceptional appearance. Another particularly beautiful catlinite pipe bowl is carved to represent an eagle's claws grasping the bowl. One pipe has a bowl of dark gray stone carved to resemble the head of a buf-

falo, with just a touch of red pigment gleaming in the corner of its eye.

An important pipe in the Cook Collection has both bowl and stem of catlinite, with only the mouthpiece of wood. This pipe is especially significant for it was smoked at Fort Laramie in 1868. That was when the U.S. Government and the Sioux signed the treaty which guaranteed the Black Hills to the Sioux "for as long as grass grows and water runs."

The collection also contains pipe tampers, used for packing smoking materials in the pipes. One of these ends whimsically with a purely decorative ring dangling atop a caged ball, all whittled carefully out of wood.

Parfleches

Among the Sioux, rawhide trunks and boxes were used to store goods in camp and while on the move. Such trunks were called parfleches. Those in the Cook Collection are of various shapes and styles of construction. Each has been painted with native pigments in striking designs.

Old-time Sioux parfleches were made of buffalo rawhide, scraped to remove flesh and hair but left untanned. Soaking for several hours makes rawhide pliable. When dry, it is again tough and stiff. The term "parfleche" is French for rawhide –

skin hard enough to deflect arrows. (The term is derived from *parer,* to parry, and *fleche,* arrow.)

Sometimes a parfleche was made by just folding the skin envelope-style while pliable. Other skins were cut and tied to make trunk-like boxes. The parfleche was lashed to the rawhide netting of the travois when people moved camp.

The Travois

The travois was a primitive vehicle used for centuries by the Plains Indians in moving camp. It consisted of an oval willow frame over which a rawhide netting was woven, making a strong, resilient platform. Two long poles, to be pulled by a horse, were next rigged like buggy shafts, except that the front ends crossed over the back of the horse and were lashed together in front of the saddle. The larger ends of the poles were left free to drag on the ground behind the horse. Bridging the space between the poles, behind the horse, the travois platform was lashed.

Household bundles and possessions, firmly tied, were placed on the travois platform. Before they had horses, Indians used dogs and smaller travois in the same way. The name "travois" was bestowed by the French fur trappers when they first arrived in the area. The Sioux name was *hunpa wanjila.*

Around the turn of the century James Cook asked one of his Indian friends to make a travois for him, in the traditional way, so that knowledge of the art would not be lost. The travois in the Cook Collection accordingly was made at his request and, to my knowledge, was never used. It may well have been made right here at Agate.

To construct this travois platform, the maker cut and peeled willow of the correct diameter. While it was still green, he then bent and lashed it into the oval form. Next, he wove the rawhide netting over it, using strips with the hair left on, softened by soaking overnight in water. When it dried, the netting was tight and strong enough to carry substantial weight. Although Plains Indians were masters of tanning, they also had many uses for rawhide, of which this is only one.

James Cook explained to visitors that this was a small travois, as he lacked space in the house for one of full size, which would be half again as large. This size was sometimes used to transport small parcels, he said, or a child too young to walk, or possibly even a dog with young puppies.

Saddles and Horse Gear

Indian saddles in the collection have a strange look to modern eyes. Those that James Cook described as Mexican seem to be modeled after saddles used by the early Spanish explorers, their high backs and fronts ornamented with brass tacks and fringe. Where and by whom they were made is not known, but Cook thought they clearly showed influence from south of the border in form and decoration. A pair of dark stirrups with beaded design on the sides was Mexican, he said, from the time in his early youth when he worked with Mexican vaqueros in the Texas brush country.

Especially interesting are the oldest saddles made by the Sioux at a time when it took real ingenuity to fashion a usable saddle at all, considering the unpromising materials at hand. On one saddle, the rawhide cover has given away, allowing the method of construction to be seen. James Cook always pointed out this saddle to visitors, to illustrate how such saddles were made.

The two sides of the saddle were made first. Wood, when it was available, was trimmed to an appropriate shape. Sometimes, the shoulder blades of bison were used. Next, deer antler in a suitable curve was trimmed and fashioned into a front and back for the saddle. These were lashed firmly into place with rawhide strips attached through holes made in the side pieces. The whole thing was then covered with fresh rawhide cut to fit, sewed into place, and allowed to dry.

James Cook was told that Indian saddles were for the use of women when moving camp. Travois poles were lashed to the saddles. It is likely that saddles such as these were fully as uncomfortable as the old MacClellan saddles of the cavalry, if not worse. Warriors avoided them, Cook explained to visitors, and presumably the women did also except when moving camp. Customarily, warriors went into battle or on a hunt bareback, with only a primitive hackamore looped over the horse's lower jaw and a single rein to control the horse.

More modern horse gear made and used by the Sioux included richly-beaded saddle cloths. A handsome example of these exists in the collection. There is also a horsehair bridle, an example of the skill with which some individuals used that material.

A military bridle in the collection is the one James Cook used in New Mexico during the Apache campaign in the 1880s. The bridle is a split-ear style, with German silver mountings and a spade bit. Knowing the bit to be needlessly cruel, Cook did not use it in later years except as an attractive bridle when needed for a photograph.

There is a fine braided rawhide lariat or lasso in the collection. Smooth and supple from long use, it possesses great

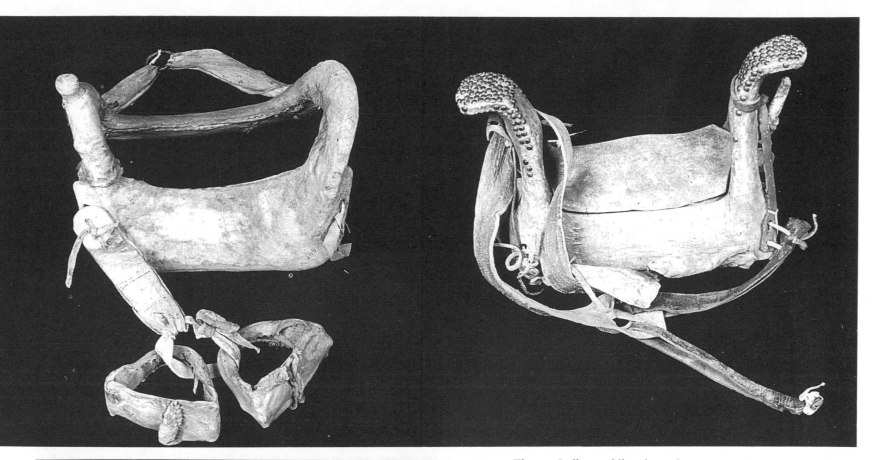

The two Indian saddles shown here represent
different styles. The bone and leather saddle at
left is crudely made, while the other is modeled
after saddles used by early Spanish explorers.
Such saddles had high fronts and backs that
were ornamented with brass tacks and fringe.

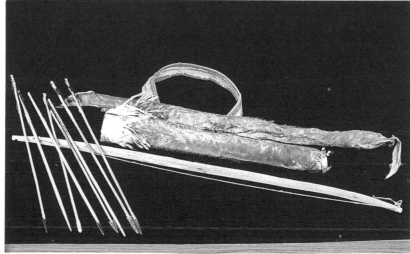

Bows, arrows, and carrying cases were
relatively simple and utilitarian.

strength. James Cook recorded the following note about an incident involving use of such a rope.

Some Easterner with a wagon train said he was going to kill the first Indian he saw. He did, but the Indians followed and made them deliver him up. They scalped and hung him right there – with a rawhide rope. That is where Rawhide (Wyoming) got its name. (18)

Lariats like this were not made by the Plains Indians. They made and used much cruder lead ropes made of heavy, unbraided hide, of which there is an example in the collection. The Sioux and Cheyenne had not developed the highly-skilled art of roping, hence they had no need of fine ropes.

Braided rawhide lariats were made and used skillfully by the Mexican cowboys with whom Cook worked in Texas. Sometimes he saw them use lariats as weapons in deadly duels.

The lasso was a dangerous fighting weapon. Many Mexicans used them in fighting duels. The idea of each fighter was to get the rope around any part of his rival's body – preferably the neck – and then whirl his horse, jerk the man out of his saddle, and drag him to death....Human life was held very cheap then by some. (19)

With incessant practice, Cook learned to rope expertly in his youth so that, lifelong, he had the ability to drop his loop exactly where it was needed.

Making a lariat required four strands of rawhide, each forty feet in length and thoroughly wet. Such strands were obtained by cutting strips from a hide in a spiral, starting at the outer edge and ending in the middle. These strands were tied to a tree and braided carefully under moderate tension. Once braided, the free end was tied to another tree, stretched, and partially dried. The maker then rolled it out under his boot, on a rock, and rubbed it full of fat before adding the honda, the loop at one end that allows the lariat loop to form.

A buggy whip with horsehair covering was made by an Indian woman of exceptional skill, a past master in the use of horsehair. Execution of the design she visualized required black horsehair, white horsehair, and white horsehair dyed into three colors. Ancient natural pigments were used for dying the hair flame-red, green, and yellow. The buggy whip in the collection was highly colorful when new, but it has lost much of its color now after more than 100 years.

In the design scheme the maker was following, the buggy whip was divided into five parts, each separated from the other by little sprays of horsehair fringe. In the largest section, at the base, all five colors were used. In each successive part, one of the colors was dropped from the design. Thus, the next to last section is only black and white. The final section at the tip was to have been braided in all black hair. Unfortunately, the artist went blind at that point and the work was never finished.

Ghost Shield, Tom-Tom, and Flutes

The ghost shield is made of rawhide ("parfleche" to the French Canadian fur trappers, or "skin that can deflect arrows"). Many rawhide ghost shields were covered with soft deerskin, tanned and appropriately decorated. Some were covered with muslin, as is true of one in the Cook Collection. Ghost shields were made with a leather strap at the back that permitted the wearer to protect either the front or the back of his body.

Ghost shields were supposed to protect the wearer from harm in battle, so James Cook was told. Beyond any supernatural powers such a shield might be thought to possess, however, it is obvious that the practical Sioux wanted the arrow-deflecting toughness of rawhide for a base, as an additional safety measure.

The tom-tom is the classic drum of the Sioux, always used to accompany dancing. It is made with a wooden frame over which rawhide has been stretched and pegged around the rim. The drumstick has a short wooden handle and a head of tanned skin, stuffed – probably with milkweed silk or cattail down – to soften the sound. Visible on the head of the tom-tom is a painted buffalo. This drum was given to James Cook by the Red Cloud family about 1900. It was used for dances around the bonfire for many years at Agate, including the times when Cook's grandchildren took part.

I well remember waiting at the door as a small child, dressed in a little Indian suit that had been made for my uncle, ready for the dance. Glimmering in the distance, a camp fire was already burning, and I glimpsed the dancers gathering. Peeking past my grandfather, I watched overawed as Jack Red Cloud strode majestically toward us in his finery, come to get the tom-tom so the dance could begin.

He stood in the doorway for a moment, looming enormously tall, stern, and a little frightening in his unfamiliar garb. Then he took the tom-tom and was gone. In the distance we heard its beat begin and the voices of the singers join in. Light from the bonfire flickered up into the leaves of the trees that arched over the dance, casting fantastic shadows as the young men moved with abandon and the

women circled, chanting and quietly stamping.

We hurried after and soon joined the circle around the camp fire. My sister and I were just getting into the swing of the women's step and were finding it rather tame. Suddenly, to our amazement and surely as a rare courtesy, one of the men invited us to join him and the others in the center. In our two little-boy suits, I suppose we did not look out of place. I will always remember my feeling of triumph at being allowed to join the dancing in the center of the ring and to dance as wildly as I liked, as the men and boys did.

Other than the tom-tom, the only musical instruments in the collection are three Indian flutes. One was played transversely, much like a modern flute in that respect. It is slim, made of a piece of hollowed-out branch of remarkably even diameter. The bark of the branch has been removed in evenly spaced segments around the body of the flute, thus producing a striking visual effect with alternating rings of bark and bare branch.

The other two flutes are played like a recorder, by blowing in a mouthpiece at one end. One is made of a length of brass pipe, to which a wooden mouthpiece has been fitted. The other end is tipped with a wooden carving of a bird's head. The third flute is larger in

diameter and was made in two halves that were first hollowed out and then brought together again. A loosely-attached, carved piece of wood is held on the side with a tie. The far end is ornamented with a long, twisted cord of sinew to which is tied a tuft of "breath feathers." The body of this flute was originally stained a light green.

War Clubs

War clubs used in this region were as varied as the makers, themselves, were individual. Still, clubs can be seen to fall into two basic categories. There were (1) clubs intended for serious use in combat and (2) clubs created solely for dances and ceremony.

War clubs intended as serious weapons were, above all, strongly constructed. They were of trim, businesslike design. A relatively small, but substantial, stone head was smoothed down, the ends slightly pointed, and an incised slot made that circled the middle. A hole was drilled in this slot to accept the handle, deep enough to make a strong joint. The handle itself, cut from the toughest wood to be found, was of a length judged to suit the owner. Once the handle was fitted into the hole, it was lashed into place with fresh, new rawhide thongs that circled the stone head and held it firmly in the slot provided. Finally, the handle was covered with rawhide stitched into place while wet and allowed to dry, reinforcing the handle. In hand-to-hand combat, the Sioux warrior armed with a well-made war club was a formidable opponent.

Ornamental clubs were intended only for ceremony. Often the head, though handsome in itself, was too heavy for the handle. Or, it might have been made of lightweight material, such as horn, that would not do for combat. Some of the most attractive war clubs in the Cook Collection were intended for ceremonial use. One such club is made of polished, greenish-black, jade-like stone at the ends, and frosted with a wide band of clear calcite crystals in the middle. The maker of this club must have been delighted to have this unique material to work with. It would be difficult to swing this beautiful war club in earnest because of the weight of the head; but, its appearance is superb. One of Red Cloud's old warriors (Minihuha, also known as Mini Lee Ha) gave this war club to James Cook about 1878. (20)

Another ceremonial club is of grey stone carved like the head of a mountain sheep. Complete with beaded handle and ornamental tassel, it is clearly not intended for warfare. A second war club is also carved to resemble the head of a mountain sheep.

The head of this club, of sandstone in a soft red, was carved with great talent and finesse. Entirely without ornament, the handle reinforced with rawhide stained to match the stone, it is a handsome design and a formidable weapon.

Two ceremonial war clubs in the collection have catlinite (pipestone) heads with inlays of polished lead. Although strongly made, these are too light for serious use in combat.

Old Sioux warriors, when they visited Agate, told many stories of hunts and battles in which they had taken part years before. One battle recalled by many was the defeat of Captain Fetterman at Fort Phil Kearny, Wyoming, in 1866. Against the express instructions of his commanding officer, Fetterman and his detail were lured over a ridge where an overwhelming number of Sioux warriors lay in wait. Fetterman and his command of 80 men were wiped out. Fetterman was killed by the Sioux warrior American Horse, in hand-to-hand combat, a war club against a saber. Years later, American Horse gave that war club to James Cook and told him the following story of the battle, vouched for by Red Cloud and others who were there. (21)

Fetterman was armed with revolver and saber; American Horse with bow and arrows, war club, and knife. As the two charged each other, riding their horses at full speed, other Indians stayed out of the way to watch. At close range, Fetterman fired, but the pistol snapped.

American Horse then discarded bow and arrow and met Fetterman's saber with his war club. The impact broke the handle of the club but deflected the saber blow and knocked them both to the ground where American Horse finished Fetterman with a knife. American Horse replaced the broken handle and later brought the war club to James Cook.

This war club is made of fine-grained, dark stone, with a well-polished surface. Its form is bluntly rounded, short and chunky. The longish handle is strengthened and protected by a neatly-sewn rawhide cover, and the whole is devoid of any ornament.

Bows and Arrows

Utilitarian bows made by Sioux and Cheyenne Indians for hunting and warfare were usually of ash, a wood of great resilience and strength. Another tree that provided excellent wood for bows was the osage orange. This small hedgerow tree was called bois d'arc (wood of bows) by the French fur trappers who were among the earliest white men to enter this area. The local place name Bodark remains as a contraction of the French.

Osage orange is native to the eastern

These war clubs were used for ceremonial purposes. They illustrate the diversity of decoration used and at the same time convey the impression that they could be used to inflict damage on an enemy when necessary. Clubs used for ceremony, however, were not as sturdily constructed as those used for combat.

half of Nebraska, where the elevation is lower and the climate more damp than the western half. Acquiring osage orange wood for bows meant trading or else taking a trip somewhat out of their usual territory, but the wood evidently had the required qualities to make it worth the effort.

Once shaped from the chosen wood, the bows were strung with twisted sinew. Arrows were then made, using wood as straight as possible for the shafts. Arrows were finished with notch and feathers at one end and point at the other. Before the arrival of white men, arrows were tipped with bone points. Iron or steel were used after they became available. Some arrows in the collection have bone points while others have steel points. An otter-skin quiver and tools needed for straightening and sanding arrows are also present.

Medicine Bow, Medicine Charms

James Cook unfailingly called particular attention to the medicine bow when he conducted visitors through the museum. He pointed out that bows intended for war and hunting were without ornament, efficiently shaped to shoot far and straight. On the other hand, the medicine bow was shaped and painted in a way intended to increase its potency in warding off

natural disasters that threatened the tribe. He pointed out that medicine arrows were tipped with stone points, unlike arrows for war and hunting. Cook described in the following manner how the Medicine Man used the bow and arrows.

Natural disasters and circumstances outside the ordinary activities of hunting and warfare required the Medicine Man to act. If, for example, an epidemic threatened the tribe, he would call on his knowledge to influence events favorably. Among the tools he could use to parry such a threat was the medicine bow, handled ceremoniously and shot in the direction thought appropriate for the menace. Or, if a severe storm threatened, the Medicine Man would shoot a medicine arrow at the storm cloud, hoping thereby to deflect its full fury from the camp.

Nicely-chipped stone points such as the Medicine Man used to tip his arrows were made by prehistoric peoples. Tribal members found them, just as we do today, and took them to the Medicine Man for his use. To this day they are found occasionally, scattered throughout western Nebraska. Old-time Sioux and Cheyenne leaders told James Cook that their people did not make stone points themselves. They believed the points had been "thrown

down" in thunderstorms by the Great Spirit, for use of the Medicine Men.

Harold Cook recorded the following observations on this matter.

Our modern Indians of the plains insist that they do not know, and never have known, as far back as their traditions reach, the art of making arrow- and spearheads from stone. They used them when they found them, to be sure, and have some very queer ideas as to how they were made, but before they could secure iron from the white man, they depended almost entirely upon bone for their arrow- and spearheads. (22)

The few medicine charms in the Cook Collection are varied and individual, relying on the natural materials available. In the one mentioned previously, tips of deer or antelope hooves and horns are strung together on a thong, like little horn bells, together with wild plum pits. In another, the bulbous root of wild turnip (*Psoralea esculenta*) is used. The underground tuber of Indian turnip was gathered and dried for food, later either soaked until soft enough to eat, or pounded up and added as thickening to other foods. The tuber, which is encased in a rough, brown skin, dries when peeled to a smooth, whitish ovoid. Indians then wrapped the short length of stem attached to each with dyed porcupine quills. Two or three of these, tied together and decorated with a tuft of feather, made a charm. Still another charm employs the hook-like end of a pronghorn horn and a beautifully-chipped stone spear point along with feathers, all on a thong.

"The White Man's God"

A wooden butter bowl in the collection is all that is known to have survived from an early wagon train that was destroyed by the Indians. An old warrior gave it to James Cook about 1900.

The warrior had been a child at the time the wagon train was attacked. Because he was young, he was not allowed to take part, but watched the entire encounter from the vantage point of high ground. Having killed the emigrants and removed all useful livestock, guns, knives, and ammunition, the Indians burned the wagons with all other possessions, saving only this butter bowl.

James Cook pointed out to visitors that the bowl is made of curly maple with a knot left on the rim. To this knot a thong was attached by which to hang it up. Strangely enough, the bowl was saved because of this knot. Whoever made the bowl had seen, in the knot, a resemblance to the head of an animal. Perhaps to amuse himself, he chose to deepen the "eyes" and add a hint of a mouth before he called it finished.

When the old warrior brought this bowl to Agate, he told James Cook that it had been his father who found it while hastily searching through the ruined wagon train before it was set afire. His father supposed the carved head represented the white man's god. He thought that to destroy it would offend his own god, so he did not burn it. Instead, he took it with him and preserved it. The family had kept the bowl until, many years later, the son gave it to James Cook.

Such rigid bowls as this were not used by the Sioux in their nomadic lives. When a bowl was needed in which to pound the seeds of chokecherries and other fruits to make pemmican, the Indians used heavy rawhide bowls made of buffalo hide. Rawhide is relatively lightweight and could be partly folded in moving. It is easy to imagine that the alien wooden butter bowl may have been used for many things in camp during its sojourn with the Sioux, but they must have found it a terrible nuisance when moving.

It has been suggested that this bowl resembles a Menominee feast bowl from Wisconsin or Minnesota. However, nothing is known about the white emigrants who were carrying it when they were overwhelmed, or from whence they came. For that reason,

who the maker of this bowl may have been – even his race or the region where he lived – must remain a mystery.

James H. Cook with the maple butter bowl which the Indians misunderstood to be a religious icon of white society. Photo taken in 1930.

Ogallala (sic) Camp
Minni Tanka River
May 13, 1908

Mr. James H. Cook
    (Wambli Cigala)
        Agate, Sioux County, Nebraska

My Old Friend:–

My son Jack and his family and all of my sub chiefs that are now here to visit you – would like to see the Painting that you had made of me in your room many years ago, by a girl friend of your family that was visiting you, I want you to always own and keep that picture – as long as you live, and then let your oldest son have it to keep. Then I am sure my children and their children can always go and look at the face of one of the last of the old Chiefs that lived before the white men came to take our lands and turn us from the old trails we had followed for so many hundreds of years. I will soon go to join my old friends and now on my last visit to you my friend I want to say through my nephew and interpreter Mr. Phillip Romero that in you I think my people will always find a true friend and I want them to listen to your words of counsel. I shake hands with you and put my mark on this letter to you.

Letter from Red Cloud to James H. Cook, dated May 13, 1908, on the great Chief's last visit to Agate.

	Chief Red Cloud	X	his mark
	Jack Red Cloud		
	Chief Red Bear	X	his mark
	Chief Runs Above	X	his mark
	Chief Walking Bull	X	his mark
Witnesses	Phillip Romero		
	Mary E. Graham		
	S.C.D. Bassett		

Ultimately, the Cook Collection of Indian artifacts adds up to several hundred individual objects that evoke the long-ago lives of these early Americans. The objects range from deadly serious tools of war and hunting to equipment for light-hearted celebrations. Some were decorated solely as a means of artistic expression, though a particular object might have had a use apart from decoration. Some are games like that which employed carved pits of wild plums, and some call for athletic skill. One of these is the game in which a notched hoop was rolled past a player who attempted to stop it with a thrown spear.

In this account, some of the more notable objects in the collection have been described, their use and history retold, as they were related to James Cook by Indian friends who brought them to him. For sixty years, these stories were told, during the lifetime of James Cook and, after him, of his son, Harold. Thousands of people over that period of time visited the Cook Museum of Natural History in the ranch house at Agate and each one received a personal tour of the collections. Especially in the early years, many visitors remarked that they had never visited a museum before.

In 1968, after both James and Harold Cook were gone, the collection was donated to the National Park Service for display at Agate Fossil Beds National Monument. A condition of the gift was that a suitable museum would be built and the artifacts kept there. In 1965, prior to the time of the donation, Congress had passed legislation that enabled a national monument to be built at Agate, and development began. Finally, in 1992, a modern museum building was completed at Agate Fossil Beds National Monument, on a site four miles east of Agate Springs Ranch, close by the fossil quarries.

The new museum will display examples of mammalian fossils found in the quarries. Included are the small rhinoceros and two giants, the claw-toed, giraffe-like Moropus, and the giant hog, Dinohyus. Fossils of the carnivorous bear-dog will also be on display.

There too, for the first time in a generation, visitors will again be able to see the Cook Collection of Indian artifacts. It is my hope that they will gain a broader understanding of the successful Indian community that flourished on the Plains before the white man came, and will recognize the importance of James Cook's vision in preserving significant aspects of that community. I particularly hope that future visitors will appreciate the foresight shown by Cook's Indian friends, those many years ago, when they brought to him for safekeeping this legacy of their former lives.

REFERENCES

Numbers in this list correspond with numbers appearing in the text beside materials quoted or otherwise referenced. The list begins at the front of the book and runs to the end.

(1) Letter from Harold J. Cook to Gene Price, dated January 30, 1960. Copy in Cook papers collection. Paraphrased and abbreviated from page 2 of sheets appended to letter.

(2) Letter from Kate G. Cook to her sister, Clara G. Heath, dated May 10, 1908. Cook papers collection.

(3) Letter from Eleanor Barbour Cook to her parents, Dr. and Mrs. E.H. Barbour, dated June 1914. Nebraska State Museum archives. Paraphrased and abbreviated. Printed in *NEBRASKAland* Magazine, May 1989, p. 40.

(4) Letter from Kate G. Cook to her sister, Clara G. Heath, dated May 10, 1908. Cook papers collection.

(5) Notebook No. 17, Box 86, Cook papers collection, Entry No. 21, dated February 22, 1938.

(6) Notebook No. 17, Box 86, Cook papers collection, Entry No. 32, dated February 22, 1938.

Paraphrased and abbreviated.

(7) Letter from Harold J. Cook to Gene Price, dated December 18, 1953.

(8) Card catalog of exchange listings for Paleontology/Geology reports, kept by Harold J. Cook. Cook papers collection. See also A-142, card file, Cook papers collection.

(9) *Trees, Shrubs and Woody Vines of the Southwest,* by Robert A. Vines, p. 568.

(10) *Tales of the 0 4 Ranch,* by Harold J. Cook, p. 221.

(11) Notebook No. 17, Box 86, Cook papers collection, Entry Nos. 36, 38, and 28. Also see *Fifty Years on the Old Frontier* by James H. Cook, p. 6. (1991 edition)

(12) Notebook No. 17, Box 86, Cook papers collection, Entry No. 16.

(13) Undated fragment of handwritten manuscript by James H. Cook, titled "Indian's Methods of Tanning Hides of Buffalo and Other Animals," typed by Dorothy C. Meade, March 1985. See also *Fifty Years on the Old Frontier* by James H. Cook, p. 109-110. (1991 edition)

(14) *Fifty Years on the Old Frontier* by James H. Cook, p. 180. (1991 edition)

(15) *Fifty Years on the Old Frontier* by James H. Cook, p. 180. (1991 edition)

(16) Letter from Eleanor Barbour Cook to her parents, Dr. and Mrs. E.H. Barbour, dated June 1914, printed in *NEBRASKAland* Magazine, May 1989, p. 40.

(17) Notebook No. 17, Box 86, Cook papers collection, Entry No. 37.

(18) Notebook No. 17, Box 86, Cook papers collection, Entry No. 1.

(19) *Fifty Years on the Old Frontier* by James H. Cook, p. 77. (1991 edition)

(20) Notebook No. 17, Box 86, Cook papers collection, Entry No. 39.

(21) *Tales of the 0 4 Ranch* by Harold J. Cook, p. 162.

(22) Article by Harold J. Cook, 1911, in *Records of the Past* Magazine (Records of the Past Exploration Society), Washington, D.C., Vol. X (Nov.-Dec.), Part VI, p. 339.

Cook, Harold J. 1969. *Tales of the 0 4 Ranch*. Univ. of Nebraska Press, Lincoln. 221 p.

Cook, James H. 1984. *Longhorn Cowboy*. 2d ed. Univ. of Oklahoma Press, Norman. 241 p.

_____. 1991. *Fifty Years on the Old Frontier*. 3d ed. Univ. of Oklahoma Press, Norman. 253 p.

Vines, Robert A. 1960. *Trees, Shrubs and Woody Vines of the Southwest*. Univ. of Texas Press, Austin. 1104 p.

James H. Cook assembled the collection of Indian artifacts which bears his name. Information in the paragraphs which follow is provided to help the reader gain a more complete understanding of this man and members of his immediate family.

James Henry Cook

Born at Kalamazoo, Michigan, 1857; died at Agate, Nebraska, 1942.

Cowboy, hunter, Indian fighter, Indian friend, Army scout (Geronimo campaign), self-educated, author of two books *(Fifty Years on the Old Frontier* and *Longhorn Cowboy,* both still in print) and numerous magazine articles; maintained a museum in his ranch home for many years; member of the Cowboy Hall of Fame.

James Cook had one brother, John Franklin Cook, who was born in 1856 and died in 1941. John F. Cook was long-time postmaster at Agate. He lived at Agate Springs Ranch in his own house until his death.

They were sons of British Captain Henry (Harry) Cook, whose family tradition held that he was descended from the great Navigator, Capt. James Cook.

James H. Cook married Kate Graham in 1886.

Kate Graham

Born at Three Rivers, Michigan, 1868; died at Lincoln, Nebraska, 1960.

Daughter of Dr. Elisha B. Graham and Mary Eliza Hutchison Graham, founders in 1879 of the 0 4 Ranch (subsequently renamed Agate Springs Ranch). Dr. and Mrs. Graham were originally from New York state. He practiced medicine there and in Michigan before moving to Cheyenne, Wyoming. Kate Graham had a sister, Clara, who was six years older.

In 1887, James and Kate bought the 0 4 Ranch from her parents when their first son, Harold J. Cook, was six weeks old. In 1898, their second son, John Graham Cook, was born at Fort Robinson, Nebraska. John lived at the ranch house until he died in 1918, at Lincoln, Nebraska.

Kate's parents separated and eventually divorced. Dr. Graham moved to California where he operated a vineyard. Kate's mother, Mary, lived at the ranch with the Cook family for many years. She later moved to California but continued to spend summers at Agate. Mary Graham was the first postmaster at Agate, Nebraska.

In 1884, when James and Kate were horseback riding, they found what would become the Agate Fossil Quarries. James informed the scientific community about the fossils after he became owner of the ranch. The quarry section remained government land, part of the open range used by the ranch, until son Harold filed for a homestead there when he reached the age of 21 (in 1908).

In 1908, Kate Graham Cook had a mental breakdown and spent the remainder of her 92 years in the state mental hospital in Lincoln.

Harold James Cook
Born at Cheyenne, Wyoming, 1887; died at Scottsbluff, Nebraska, 1962.

Harold J. Cook had an active and productive career as a geologist and paleontologist. Educated at the University of Nebraska and Columbia University, he did much work in connection with Early Man sites, notably the original Folsom quarry site in New Mexico and the Eden Valley site. He was Curator of Vertebrate Paleontology at the Denver Museum and was author of many publications. He was subsequently involved in oil geology in several states, at all times continuing to run Agate Springs Ranch, often *in absentia*. He was awarded an honorary doctorate from the South Dakota School of Mines in 1960.

Harold Cook married Eleanor Barbour in 1910.

Eleanor Barbour
Born at New Haven, Connecticut, 1889; died at Pullman, Washington, 1976.

Eleanor Barbour was the daughter of Dr. Erwin H. Barbour, Director of the Nebraska State Museum and of the Nebraska Geological Survey. He also served as chairman of the Geology Department at the University of Nebraska and was considered the "Father of Nebraska Paleontology." He had a Ph.D. from Yale University and was one of the first paleontologists to collect at the Agate quarries after they opened in 1904. He authored hundreds of publications.

Eleanor was a geologist, scholar, and musician. After 1923, she taught geology and English for 18 years at the college in Chadron, Nebraska, played in the college orchestra, and founded the first museum at the college.

Harold and Eleanor Barbour Cook were the parents of four daughters: Margaret, Dorothy, Winifred, and Eleanor. Harold, Eleanor, and the four girls lived in the ranch house at Agate with Harold's father, James H. Cook.

The daughters were taught at home on the ranch for several years. Later education occurred in Chadron and Lincoln, Nebraska. All attended the University of Nebraska, where Dorothy and Eleanor received degrees. Margaret graduated from Chadron College, and Winifred graduated and earned the M.A. degree at Eastern Washington State University in Cheney, Washington.

All the daughters married and had children, and two of the daughters (Dorothy and Winifred) married geologists. All four Cook daughters were musicians.

Harold and Eleanor Cook separated in 1923 and then divorced in 1927. Harold then married Margaret Crozier in 1927 and they lived at Agate Springs Ranch for the remainder of their lives. Harold died in 1962, Margaret in 1968.

In 1961, the National Park Service proposed creating a National Monument of the fossil quarries. After Harold's death, his widow pushed hard for the Monument to be formed. Congress passed enabling legislation in 1965. In 1968, Margaret Crozier Cook donated the Indian collection to the National Park Service, stipulating that it was to be placed on display in a suitable museum that would be built at Agate. She also put together *Tales of the O 4 Ranch,* a book taken from tapes made by Harold Cook about his boyhood and youth.

After the death of Margaret Crozier Cook, the four daughters, who had inherited the ranch from their father, formed a family corporation which has since continued to operate the ranch.

Dorothy Cook Meade is one of the four grand-daughters of James H. Cook, who assembled the items which comprise the Cook Collection of Indian artifacts. Her father, Harold J. Cook, was one of James and Kate Cook's two sons.

Mrs. Meade's intimate relationship with the Cook Collection goes back to her childhood. She lived in the ranch house at Agate Springs Ranch, with her parents, sisters, and grandfather, until 1923 when she was ten years old. Subsequently, she visited the ranch many summers.

Dorothy Cook earned the B.A. degree in zoology at the University of Nebraska in 1934. For the next three years, she taught public school music in Chadron, Nebraska. In 1937, she married Grayson Meade, a graduate student of geology at the University of Chicago. They lived 14 years in Texas and then 20 years in Calgary, Alberta, Canada. Mrs. Meade pursued her interests in music, taking active roles in music education as well as performing with several orchestras and chamber music ensembles.

In 1972, Dorothy and Grayson Meade returned to Nebraska and they took over management of Agate Springs Ranch for the family corporation. It has been their home ever since.

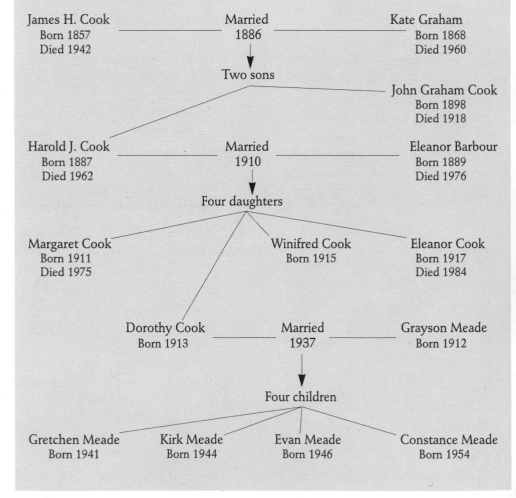

A COOK FAMILY GENEALOGY

James H. Cook
Born 1857
Died 1942

Married
1886

Kate Graham
Born 1868
Died 1960

Two sons

John Graham Cook
Born 1898
Died 1918

Harold J. Cook
Born 1887
Died 1962

Married
1910

Eleanor Barbour
Born 1889
Died 1976

Four daughters

Margaret Cook
Born 1911
Died 1975

Winifred Cook
Born 1915

Eleanor Cook
Born 1917
Died 1984

Dorothy Cook
Born 1913

Married
1937

Grayson Meade
Born 1912

Four children

Gretchen Meade
Born 1941

Kirk Meade
Born 1944

Evan Meade
Born 1946

Constance Meade
Born 1954